Connect to Conquer

A Student's Journey in Professional Networking

SANATH NAIR

For my cherished wife, whose love guides me and our son, the light of our lives.

This book is a small reflection of the endless inspiration you both infuse into my life

Contents

Preface

The digital age has ushered in a new era of communication, fundamentally transforming how we connect, collaborate, and create. As traditional boundaries blur and the world becomes more interconnected, the power of networking has become more immense than ever. **"Connect to Conquer: A Student's Journey in Professional Networking"** has been written with this understanding, a passion for networking, and a commitment to help you navigate the evolving landscape of networking as effectively and efficiently as possible.

The concept of creating a comprehensive book on Business Networking for Students took form during the later phases of my initial book on Corporate Transition. In that book, I touched upon this subject briefly, exploring it through the lens of four determined students and their mentors.

In this book, we venture beyond conventional approaches and dive deep into the different perspectives, bringing to light new strategies, insights, and tools that are reshaping the networking landscape. This book serves as your compass, guiding you through an uncharted terrain filled with opportunities and challenges, equipping you with the knowledge to adapt, evolve and thrive.

This is not just a book about networking—it's about embracing change, nurturing innovation, and fostering a culture of lifelong learning. It is about understanding the true essence of networking, not merely as a tool for professional growth.

☐

Introduction

In the fast-paced, competitive world of academia and professional development, students often wonder how to stand out, make valuable connections, and secure a bright future. Connect to Conquer: A Student's Journey in Professional Networking is a comprehensive guide designed to help students navigate the intricate networking world and leverage it for personal and professional growth. In this book, we will explore the art and science of networking, providing practical tips, real-life examples, and step-by-step strategies to build a robust network that will serve as the foundation for your success.

Building a professional network as a student can be a transformative experience. It's not just about collecting business cards or LinkedIn connections; it's about forming meaningful relationships that can shape your academic, personal, and professional life. We'll dive deep into the intricacies of networking, from understanding its significance to learning how to harness the power of social media, in-person events, and one-on-one interactions.

In the following chapters, I will take you on a journey through networking, offering guidance on creating an impactful elevator pitch, mastering the art of small talk, and building a compelling personal brand. We'll also address students' challenges when networking and provide strategies to overcome them.

Whether you're aiming for a successful career in a traditional corporate setting, hoping to launch your entrepreneurial venture, or simply seeking to grow, this book will equip you with the knowledge and skills you need to make networking an integral part of your life. By the end of this comprehensive guide, you'll be well on your way to creating a robust professional network that will open doors, provide support, and drive your success.

So, if you are ready to start this journey of self-discovery and professional growth through networking, let's begin with Chapter 1, where we'll explore the importance of networking for students.

The Importance of Networking for Students

In today's fast-paced, interconnected world, networking has become an increasingly critical skill for students. It goes beyond accumulating academic achievements; it plays a pivotal role in securing a prosperous future. Networking acts as a bridge, connecting the knowledge gained through education with real-world opportunities and fostering professional growth and personal development. By building meaningful connections and nurturing relationships, students can tap into a vast network of resources, mentors, and potential collaborators who can provide guidance and support and open doors to new and exciting ventures. Thus, the importance of networking cannot be overstated, as it catalyses unlocking a world of possibilities and shaping a successful and fulfilling journey.

The Networking Paradox

Many students, particularly those new to the professional world, need help with networking. It frequently conjures visions of packed conferences, where the urge to network and engage in diminutive conversation can feel overpowering. Fear of rejection may also be present, as one is concerned about not being fascinating enough or having enough to contribute.

However, it is essential to recognise that networking does not have to be daunting or insincere. When approached with the right mindset, it can be an authentic and fulfilling process. Networking is about building genuine relationships, connecting with like-minded individuals, and finding opportunities for collaboration and growth. It is a chance to learn from others, share experiences, and expand one's professional network.

Students can overcome their initial reservations about networking by viewing it as an opportunity to interact, learn, and explore new options. Whether attending industry events, joining professional organisations, or reaching out to peers and mentors, networking can open doors to new opportunities, provide valuable insights, and help students navigate their career paths confidently. So, instead of seeing networking as daunting, let us view it as an exciting adventure filled with potential and possibilities.

The Power of Connections

Networking is a powerful practice that allows you to tap into the vast wisdom, experience, and invaluable support of those who have walked the path before you. It presents a golden opportunity to connect with seasoned professionals, mentors, and like-minded peers who can offer valuable insights, guidance, and potential job opportunities that may propel your career to new heights. Building these meaningful connections can be the key that unlocks doors that would otherwise remain closed, opening a world of possibilities and paving the way for your continuous growth and success.

Building a Bridge to the Future

Your student years are a valuable time to gain knowledge and skills and a crucial period to start building meaningful relationships and laying the foundation for your future success. As you transition from the educational to the professional world, the network you establish during this time will become an invaluable resource for securing internships and job offers and accelerating your career growth.

The connections you make during your student years have the potential to shape your journey for years to come. These relationships can open doors to new opportunities, provide mentorship, and offer guidance as you navigate the ever-evolving professional landscape. By nurturing and expanding your network, you will have a support system offering insights, advice, and potential collaborations as you progress in your chosen field.

So, make the most of your student years by actively engaging with your peers, professors, industry professionals, and alums. Attend networking events, join relevant clubs and organisations, and clinch every chance to connect with others who share your passions and aspirations. Remember, the relationships you cultivate now can be pivotal in paving the way for a fulfilling and prosperous future.

A Continuous Learning Experience

Networking is not a one-time activity but a lifelong process constantly evolving alongside personal and professional growth. As you cross different phases of life, your network will naturally adapt to your shifting needs, aspirations, and ambitions. It will be a valuable resource, providing continuous personal and professional development opportunities. By nurturing and expanding your network, you open doors to new connections, collaborations, and insights that propel you towards tremendous success and fulfilment. Accept the power of networking to build genuine relationships and open up a world of opportunities.

Overcoming Common Misconceptions

Before we explore the art of networking, we must address some common misconceptions and fears that often hinder students from taking full advantage of networking opportunities. By dispelling these myths, we can empower ourselves to approach networking confidently, authentically, and clearly understand its benefits. By understanding the value of building meaningful connections and leveraging them for personal and professional growth, we can truly unlock the potential that networking holds. So, let us explore these misconceptions and fears individually and equip ourselves with the knowledge and mindset needed to thrive in networking.

Networking is Manipulative: Some students worry that networking involves using people solely for personal gain. However, networking is about building genuine and authentic relationships that are mutually beneficial. It is a chance to connect with like-minded individuals, share knowledge, collaborate, and support each other's professional growth.

It is All About Quantity: Many believe that the more connections they have, the better. However, the quality of your relationships often matters more than the quantity. Building strong and meaningful connections with a few key individuals can provide more value than having dozens of superficial ones. It is about nurturing relationships built on trust and shared interests, where both parties can genuinely support and uplift each other.

Networking is Only for Extroverts: Introverts can also be highly effective networkers. Networking is more than just being the loudest voice in the room. It is making meaningful connections through genuine interactions. Introverts often excel at listening, observing, and forming deep relationships. It is about finding your unique networking style that aligns with your personality and strengths.

It is Only About Business: Networking extends beyond professional relationships. While it is a valuable tool for career development and finding mentors, it also offers opportunities for personal growth. Networking allows you to connect with individuals who share your passions, interests, and values, fostering a sense of belonging in your chosen field. It is a chance to build a supportive community that inspires and motivates you professionally and personally.

Networking is Only for Finding Jobs: While networking can lead to job opportunities, its benefits go far beyond that. Networking provides a platform to gain knowledge, guidance, and insights from experienced professionals. It allows you to tap into a wealth of expertise, learn from others' experiences, and expand your horizons. Additionally, networking can offer personal support and encouragement during challenging times, helping you navigate the ups and downs of your career journey.

Several case studies on the importance of networking for students are worth looking into. You should begin by examining a thought-provoking study titled **"Should I be Networking? Exploring the**

importance of networking for students." This case study by Jennifer Bonds-Raacke, John Raacke, and Samantha Elliott explores the importance of networking for students. It emphasises that networking is about building and maintaining relationships, which may lead to a mutually beneficial exchange in the future. The study suggests that networking can open many doors and possibilities for students, and it is never too early to start. This study emphasises that networking goes beyond mere contact-making; it is about cultivating and nurturing relationships that can pave the way for mutually beneficial exchanges in the future. This study's key takeaway is that it is never too early for students to start networking.

Moving on, try to explore a captivating case study titled **"Learn to Love Networking"**, published in the renowned Harvard Business Review. Authored by Francesca Gino, Maryam Kouchaki, and Tiziana Casciaro, this case study presents four strategies that can make networking a more enjoyable and practical experience. Individuals can build meaningful and enduring relationships by focusing on continuous learning, finding common interests, considering what they can offer others, and finding a higher purpose in networking. The insights from this case study shed light on how someone can approach networking with a mindset of personal growth and contribution.

To provide practical guidance, you can read the informative guide titled **"How To Network In College: How To Make Connections Before You Graduate."** This Forbes Advisor article by Meghan Gallagher provides practical tips on how students can effectively network during college. This guide offers valuable information for students on networking effectively during their college years. It emphasises the importance of building a well-connected network that can provide valuable insights into career paths aligned with a student's field of study. Additionally, it gives tips on applications and leads for job opportunities that may still need to be publicly listed. The guide is a valuable resource for students seeking to maximise their networking efforts in college.

These case studies underscore the importance of networking for students and provide actionable strategies for building and maintaining a solid network. They highlight that networking involves making contacts and cultivating relationships that can lead to opportunities and mutual benefits. Moreover, they emphasise the significance of starting early and approaching networking, focusing on continuous learning, and giving rather than solely receiving. The insights gained from these case studies can serve as valuable content for the first chapter of your book, aligning perfectly with its theme of business networking.

In the following chapters, we will learn about the fascinating networking world, uncovering the common misconceptions that may hold you back. Together, we will unravel the secrets to incorporating networking as a powerful personal and professional growth tool. Get ready to unlock a treasure trove of knowledge and skills that will empower you to become a confident and authentic networker, effortlessly connecting with others and opening doors to endless opportunities.

Preparing for Successful Networking

Now that you understand the importance of networking and have dispelled some common misconceptions, it's time to prepare yourself for successful networking as a student. Focusing on thorough preparation will establish a solid foundation for forging meaningful connections and unlocking future opportunities. Whether it's researching industry events, honing your elevator pitch, or expanding your professional network, taking the time to fine-tune your networking skills will undoubtedly pay off in the long run. So, enjoy this path of preparation and equip yourself to make the most of any networking opportunity that comes your way!

Identifying Your Goals

Before you plunge into the vast networking world, take a moment to reflect on your goals and aspirations. Ask yourself, what do you truly hope to achieve through networking? Are you seeking invaluable mentorship that will propel you towards success? Are you seeking exciting job opportunities that align with your passion and expertise? Or you may yearn to expand your horizons and gain profound industry knowledge that will set you apart.

Remember that your goals guide your networking journey. They will shape your approach, paving the path for genuine connections with the people who can help you thrive and flourish. So, take the time to define your objectives and make them the driving force behind your networking efforts.

Crafting Your Brand

Your brand is not just about how you present yourself to the world; it reflects your identity, encompassing your skills, experiences, and values that set you apart. It's like a mosaic, where each piece represents a facet of your character and expertise, coming together to form a unique and compelling story. By developing a deep understanding of your brand, you gain the power to authentically connect with others and effectively showcase what you bring to the table. Further, it enables you to build meaningful relationships and create opportunities that align with your aspirations and goals. Follow the road of self-discovery and confidently articulate your brand to leave an indelible mark on both personal and professional levels.

Elevator Pitch Mastery

An elevator pitch is a concise and compelling introduction you can deliver in the time it takes to ride an elevator. It is a powerful tool for making a solid first impression in networking situations. In Chapter 5 of our book, we will understand deeper into this topic, exploring various strategies and techniques for crafting an effective elevator pitch. For now, take a moment to consider what indeed makes you stand out from the crowd and how you can artfully articulate it in a brief yet memorable way. Furthermore, your elevator pitch is your chance to highlight your unique abilities, experiences, and value, so take advantage of it!

Preparing Questions and Conversations

Engaging in meaningful conversations is essential and a crucial aspect of effective networking. Whether attending a networking event or reaching out to someone individually, preparing thoughtful questions and engaging discussion topics can significantly enhance your networking experience.

Doing so prevents awkward silences and creates a welcoming environment, fostering connections and rapport. Show genuine interest in the people you meet, actively listening to their stories and experiences. It not only helps you establish meaningful connections but also allows you to gain valuable insights and perspectives from a diverse range of individuals.

Networking is about more than just exchanging business cards or promoting your interests. It's about building genuine relationships, learning from others, and creating a network of like-minded individuals who can support and inspire you throughout your professional journey. So, take the time to prepare, engage in meaningful conversations, and seize the opportunity to connect with others on a deeper level.

Building Your Online Presence

Establishing a solid online presence is crucial in today's digital age, where virtual connections are as meaningful as face-to-face interactions. In Chapter 7, we will investigate the profound impact of online networking. But for now, take some time to refine your LinkedIn profile, ensuring it impeccably aligns with your unique personal brand and professional aspirations. Doing so will enhance accessibility and open doors to valuable connections and opportunities.

Setting Realistic Expectations

Networking is not a magical solution that guarantees instant success. It's a long-term investment in your future, built on genuine connections and meaningful interactions. By setting realistic expectations, you understand that only some interactions will lead to immediate results. However, each link you make can benefit you in the long run, whether through new opportunities, valuable insights, or lasting friendships. So, nurture your network, engage in meaningful conversations, and embrace the journey of growth and collaboration. Your efforts will surely pay off in ways you never imagined.

Developing Confidence

Confidence is a crucial and empowering factor in successful networking. It stems from believing in your abilities and recognising the value you bring to the table. When you exude confidence, you become more approachable and magnetic to others, fostering meaningful connections. In Chapter 10, we'll discuss the intricacies of networking etiquette and share invaluable best practices that will boost your confidence and elevate your networking skills to new heights. You can navigate any networking situation quickly and gracefully if you master these techniques.

The Power of Giving

Don't forget, networking goes both ways! It's not just about what you can gain from others; it's also about what you can give. You create a positive and supportive environment by being open to helping others in your network. A generous attitude can lead to more robust, authentic connections that benefit you personally and professionally. Taking the time to listen, offer advice, or provide resources shows your commitment to building meaningful relationships. So, harness the power of reciprocity and watch your network thrive!

Start with Your Existing Network

You don't have to start from scratch when starting your networking journey. Begin by contacting your friends, family, professors, and classmates. These familiar connections can be a great starting point and provide valuable introductions and advice. They can also help you navigate the professional landscape and share their experiences, giving you a head start on building a solid network. So don't hesitate to tap into these relationships as you begin your networking adventure!

Action Plan

It is critical to have a complete action plan before commencing your route to successful networking. Take the time to set specific, measurable, and achievable goals that align with your networking objectives. Consider outlining the events you plan to attend, the individuals you wish to connect with, and the skills you aim to enhance through these interactions. By having a well-defined plan, you will stay focused and motivated and increase your chances of accomplishing your networking goals.

Chapter 3 of this guide will look at how to use social media to make professional connections. But before we dive into that, it is essential to dedicate some time to prepare yourself thoroughly for the exciting networking journey that lies ahead. With the proper preparation and strategising, you will be well on your way to establishing a robust professional network that will open doors to endless opportunities and propel your career to new heights.

Leveraging Social Media for Professional Connections

In our modern digital age, social media has become a powerful tool for networking and establishing professional connections. With its widespread reach and accessibility, social media platforms offer unparalleled opportunities to connect with like-minded individuals, industry experts, and potential collaborators. Whether you want to expand your network, showcase your expertise, or stay updated with the latest industry trends, this chapter will provide valuable insights and practical guidance on effectively leveraging social media to build and nurture your professional relationships. By implementing the strategies and best practices outlined here, you will be able to harness the full potential of social media and unlock new avenues for growth and success in your career.

The Power of Social Media

Social media platforms like LinkedIn, X (Twitter), and Facebook have revolutionised how we connect with professionals and industries. They offer a virtual space to showcase your accomplishments, share valuable insights, and exhibit your passions to a vast global audience. When harnessed strategically, social media becomes a powerful tool that expands your network and facilitates meaningful connections with like-minded individuals who can contribute to your personal and professional growth. By leveraging the potential of these platforms, you can create opportunities, foster collaboration, and stay updated with the latest trends and developments in your field. Leverage the possibilities of social media to elevate your presence and unlock a world of endless possibilities!

LinkedIn: Your Professional Hub

LinkedIn, widely recognised as the ultimate platform for professional networking, is an invaluable resource for students seeking to establish connections with mentors, employers, and peers. Crafting and nurturing a robust LinkedIn profile can significantly enhance your chances of securing rewarding opportunities in your desired field. To help you optimise your LinkedIn presence, here are some essential tips and strategies to consider:

Use a professional photo: Choose a high-quality photo where you look friendly and professional. A clear and well-lit image will leave a positive impression on viewers.

Craft a compelling headline: Your headline should go beyond simply stating your job title. It should capture your unique value and expertise, showcasing what sets you apart from others in your industry. A strong and engaging headline will pique the interest of potential connections and employers.

Write a compelling summary: Your summary presents an opportunity to tell your professional story captivatingly. Utilise this section to highlight your skills, experiences, and goals, emphasising how they align with your career aspirations. Share anecdotes and insights that showcase your passion and expertise, making your profile more memorable and enticing to readers.

Showcase your achievements: Can you include specific details about your education, work experience, projects, and any notable awards or honours you have received? Highlighting your accomplishments demonstrates your competence and credibility, giving others a clear understanding of your capabilities and potential contributions.

Connect strategically: When reaching out to connect with others on LinkedIn, personalise your connection requests to establish a meaningful connection. Explain why you want to connect, highlighting common interests, shared contacts, or potential collaboration opportunities. Personalising your messages shows genuine interest and increases the likelihood of building valuable professional relationships.

X(Twitter): Engage in Industry Conversations

X(Twitter) is an exceptional platform for staying updated on the latest industry trends and engaging in meaningful conversations with professionals in your field. By actively following industry leaders, participating in relevant discussions, and consistently sharing valuable insights and experiences, you can effectively demonstrate your expertise and establish yourself as a thought leader. Additionally, by attracting like-minded individuals to your network, you can foster valuable connections and collaborations to enhance your professional growth and opportunities further. Use X (Twitter) to broaden your expertise, network, and influence in your field.

Facebook: Join Industry-Specific Groups

While Facebook is widely known for facilitating personal connections, it also provides a diverse range of industry-specific groups and communities. These groups can be an invaluable resource for professionals looking to connect with like-minded individuals in their respective fields. By joining these groups, you can engage in meaningful discussions, ask questions, and share valuable insights with others who share your interests. It not only helps you expand your network but also allows you to stay updated on the latest trends and developments within your industry.

So, don't hesitate to explore these communities and maximise their opportunities!

Personal Website or Blog

A personal website or blog can be a powerful tool for personal branding and networking. With a dedicated online space, you can showcase your thoughts, experiences, and projects related to your field of interest more comprehensively and engagingly. You will be able to demonstrate your expertise and provide a unique platform to connect with like-minded individuals interested in your work. Additionally, it allows you to establish yourself as a thought leader in your industry. It opens opportunities for collaborations, partnerships, and even potential career advancements. So, take the chance to build a solid online presence and leverage the benefits it can bring to your professional journey!

Social Media Etiquette

Maintaining professionalism on social media is crucial for building a solid personal brand. Here are some essential etiquette tips to help you navigate the digital landscape with finesse:

Be respectful: It's super important to treat others with courtesy and respect in all our interactions. How you present yourself online says a lot about who you are, so always choose your words wisely.

Share value: When you post on social media, aim to provide value to your connections. Share informative articles, insightful perspectives, and personal experiences that can enrich their knowledge or spark meaningful conversations.

Engage thoughtfully: If you join discussions or respond to comments, do so thoughtfully and constructively. Take the time to comprehend others' perspectives and contribute to the conversation in a meaningful way. It will help you establish yourself as a thoughtful and knowledgeable professional.

Avoid oversharing: While it is encouraged to share your professional journey, it is crucial to strike a balance and avoid oversharing personal information. Keep your focus on topics that are relevant to your professional goals and interests.

By adhering to these etiquette tips, you can maintain a professional and positive online presence that will leave a lasting impression on your network.

Building an Online Portfolio

Your social media profiles should be an online portfolio showcasing your skills, experiences, and accomplishments. It is crucial to regularly update your profiles to reflect your growth, new achievements, and ongoing professional development. You can attract more opportunities, connections, and collaborations by consistently maintaining an active and engaging online presence.

This chapter of my book explored the Power of leveraging social media for professional connections. To strengthen my points in this chapter, let us examine three insightful case studies that shed light on organisations' journey in developing their use of social media with employees.

The first case study, **"Use of Social Media at Work Case Studies"**, published by CIPD, presents the main themes from seven in-depth case studies. These studies provide detailed accounts of how organisations have utilised social media to create engaging and empowering workplaces. They highlight the benefits and how social media can facilitate more robust employee connections.

Next, we have **"Strengthen Your Professional Presence on Social Media"**, an article written by Michelle Gibbings, a renowned global keynote speaker and author. Gibbings offers practical tips on how to use social media to strengthen your career. She emphasises that being on a social media platform alone is not enough; what truly matters is your visibility, impact, and how these factors align with your career goals.

Lastly, we explore **"132 Social Media Case Studies - Successes and Failures"**, compiled by Susanna

Gebauer. This collection comprehensively examines both successful and failed social media activities. By studying these cases, you will gain valuable insights into the dos and don'ts of using social media for professional connections. Gebauer emphasises that the success or failure of social media activities lies not in the platform itself but in the strategies employed and the approach taken.

We will go deeper into the art of attending networking events and conferences in the following chapter. We will explore practical strategies for making meaningful connections, expanding your network, and leveraging these events to propel your career forward. But for now, remember that social media is a dynamic and powerful tool for increasing your network and reaching a broader audience. By using these platforms strategically, you can connect with professionals, engage in industry conversations, share valuable insights, and build a solid personal brand in the digital world. Accept the endless possibilities that social media provides and open new avenues for growth and achievement.

Attending Networking Events and Conferences

While social media provides an excellent platform for networking, there's no substitute for the power of face-to-face interactions. Attending networking events and conferences offers unique opportunities to connect with like-minded professionals, exchange ideas, and build meaningful relationships. These in-person gatherings allow you to immerse yourself in your chosen field, engage in insightful conversations, and stay updated with the latest trends and advancements. Whether attending industry-specific conferences or joining local networking groups, making the most of these opportunities can significantly enhance your professional growth and open doors to new possibilities. This chapter will explore the practical strategies and proven techniques to maximise your experience at these valuable in-person gatherings. So, get ready to expand your network, gain valuable insights, and make lasting connections to propel your career forward!

The Benefits of In-Person Networking

Networking events and conferences offer a multitude of advantages for students seeking to broaden their professional horizons:

Direct Connections: These events provide a unique opportunity to meet professionals, peers, and potential mentors in person. Face-to-face conversations allow for more profound understanding and rapport, forming meaningful connections.

Learning Opportunities: Networking events often feature a wide range of workshops, seminars, and keynote speakers. Attending these sessions can provide valuable insights and knowledge, helping students stay updated with industry trends and advancements. Additionally, it allows for exchanging ideas and experiences with experts in their respective fields.

Networking Niche: One of the advantages of attending networking events is the ability to focus on specific events that cater to your interests and industry. It will allow for more targeted networking, increasing the chances of making connections that align with your career goals and aspirations. Attending events tailored to your niche will enable you to connect with individuals with similar passions and professional interests.

Personal Impressions: Face-to-face interactions leave a lasting impression beyond a LinkedIn profile. Networking events provide a platform to showcase your personality, communication skills, and professionalism. Engaging in conversations, asking thoughtful questions, and actively listening can leave a positive and memorable impression on others, potentially opening doors to future opportunities.

By actively participating in networking events and conferences, students can leverage their advantages to expand their professional network, gain valuable knowledge, and make lasting connections that can positively impact their future endeavours.

Preparing for the Event

Before attending a networking event or conference, it is crucial to be well-prepared. Taking the time to plan can significantly enhance your experience and maximise the opportunities available. Here are some critical steps to consider:

Research the Event: Make sure you take the time to thoroughly research the event. It's important to dive deep and gather all the information you need. Understand its purpose, schedule, and speakers. Dive into the details and identify the sessions that align with your goals and interests. It will allow you to make the most of your time and ensure you attend the most relevant sessions.

Set Objectives: Make sure you have clear goals in mind for the event. What do you want to achieve? Are you looking to expand your professional network, find a mentor, or connect with potential employers? Clear objectives will help you stay focused and guide your interactions throughout the event.

Prepare Your Elevator Pitch

Craft a concise and compelling elevator pitch that effectively introduces yourself and highlights your strengths and areas of expertise.

Think about what makes you unique and how you can stand out in a crowd.

Practice delivering your elevator pitch beforehand to ensure confidence and clarity when interacting with others.

Make sure you pay attention to what you wear and dress appropriately for the event. Consider the formality of the event and the industry you're targeting. Professional attire builds credibility and demonstrates that you take the occasion seriously. Remember, first impressions matter, so dress in a way that reflects your professionalism and aligns with the expectations of the event.

Now, you'll be well-prepared and ready to make meaningful connections and maximise your experience at the networking event or conference.

Engaging in Meaningful Conversations

Make the most of your time at the event by engaging in meaningful conversations. Follow these helpful guidelines to ensure productive and insightful discussions that leave a lasting impact. By actively listening, asking thought-provoking questions, and sharing valuable insights, you'll foster deeper connections and create a truly enriching experience for yourself and others. So, seize the opportunity to network, learn, and grow while establishing meaningful relationships with fellow attendees.

Approach Others: Don't hesitate to take the initiative and approach fellow attendees. Most people are there to network and are open to interactions. By being confident and friendly, you can create valuable connections.

Listen Actively: When engaging in conversations, actively listen to what others say. Show genuine interest by maintaining eye contact, nodding, and asking thoughtful questions. As a result, you can build a stronger connection with them and show that you are paying attention.

Share Your Insights: Contribute to discussions by sharing your experiences, expertise, or unique insights related to the event's topics. You showcase your knowledge and contribute to the conversation's overall learning and engagement by offering valuable input.

Follow-Up: Follow up with the people you connected with after the event. Send a personalised message expressing appreciation for the conversation and your desire to stay in touch. This gesture shows your professionalism and genuine interest in building a lasting relationship beyond the event.

By following these guidelines, you can make the most of your event experience and create meaningful connections that can lead to new opportunities.

Navigating Networking Challenges

Attending networking events can be overwhelming, particularly for introverted individuals who may find themselves outside their comfort zones. However, navigating these events can become more manageable and enjoyable with the right strategies and mindset. By implementing helpful tips and techniques, introverts can confidently engage with others, build meaningful connections, and make the most of these valuable networking opportunities. So, let's explore some practical approaches to help you navigate common challenges and thrive in networking events!

Overcoming Shyness: If you feel shy in social situations, a helpful strategy is to start with small groups. Gradually exposing yourself to social interactions can build your confidence over time. Take small steps and challenge yourself to engage in conversations and group activities. As you gain confidence, you can gradually broaden your social circle and easily handle larger gatherings.

Dealing with Rejection: Just remember that not every interaction will lead to a connection, and that's totally fine. Rejection is a natural part of socialising and doesn't reflect your worth or value. Instead of taking it personally, try to reframe rejection as an opportunity for growth and learning. Use it to refine your approach, learn from the experience, and move forward with resilience and optimism.

Exiting Conversations: You may be in conversations that do not align with your goals or interests. In such situations, it's perfectly acceptable to leave the conversation politely. You can express your desire to meet other attendees or engage in discussions more aligned with your interests. It's essential to prioritise your time and energy in a way that helps you make the most of any social gathering.

Building Meaningful Connections: While it can be tempting to focus on the quantity of connections you make, it's important to prioritise quality over quantity. Instead of meeting as many people as possible, focus on building meaningful relationships with individuals with similar interests, values, or goals. These connections are more likely to be fulfilling and impact your personal and professional life. Take the time to engage in deeper conversations, show genuine interest in others, and nurture these connections for long-term benefits. One meaningful relationship can be more valuable than dozens of superficial ones.

The Power of Follow-Up

You must still complete your work after attending a networking event or a conference. Following up is a crucial step in maintaining and nurturing the connections you've made. Take the time to send a personalised email, connect on social media platforms like LinkedIn or X(Twitter), or even schedule a coffee meeting with those individuals who align with your professional goals and aspirations. Doing so solidifies the connections you've established and creates opportunities for collaboration and mutual growth.

I have selected three case studies highlighting academic conferences' benefits for this chapter. These case studies shed light on the significance of attending meetings for professional connections and provide practical strategies for maximising these opportunities. They emphasise that conferences are about sharing research and building relationships, staying updated on new developments, and gaining visibility in your field.

The first case study, **"10 Benefits of Attending Academic Conferences"**, was written by Elizabeth

George and published on Researcher. Life delves into the advantages of attending academic conferences. It emphasises the importance of sharing research with peers, enhancing presentation skills, and engaging in insightful discussions on the latest happenings in your field of study. The critical insight from this case study is that academic conferences offer valuable opportunities to learn about cutting-edge research, meet new people, and build strong professional relationships within your field.

The second case study, titled **"The Great Benefits of Attending Academic Conferences"**, written by Miguel Otero-Iglesias and published on UACES, provides insights into the benefits of attending academic conferences. Attending conferences can help researchers stay informed about scientific developments, discover career-changing prospects, and establish robust working relationships. The key takeaway from this case study is that attending academic conferences early on in your PhD journey and continuing to do so at least once a year can significantly benefit your career.

The third case study, titled **"A Researcher's Guide to Making the Most of Academic Conferences"**, is a guide published by Enago Academy. It highlights the importance of conferences in an academic career and showcases the valuable opportunities they provide for networking, sharing research, and learning about new developments. The critical insight from this case study is that conferences serve as a platform for researchers to present their ongoing research, fostering a more open and collaborative scientific community.

I recommend anyone reading this book to go through it, especially if you are a student or a graduate. These insights will offer you practical guidance and inspire you to make the most of these opportunities, ultimately helping them succeed in their academic and professional journeys.

In the next chapter, I will discuss crafting an effective elevator pitch, a vital tool for making a solid and impactful first impression during networking events and conferences. Mastering the art of delivering a compelling elevator pitch can help you stand out from the crowd and leave a lasting impression on potential contacts and collaborators. However, for now, always remember that in-person networking remains a powerful and invaluable way to create genuine connections, expand your professional network, and open doors to new and exciting opportunities. Acknowledge the value of face-to-face encounters and grab every opportunity to build authentic relationships in your sector.

Building Effective Elevator Pitches

Your elevator pitch is crucial to making a solid and memorable first impression at networking events, conferences, or any other networking opportunity. It is a concise yet impactful introduction that captures who you are, what you do, and the value you bring.

Crafting an effective elevator pitch requires careful thought and consideration. This chapter will guide you through creating a compelling pitch that resonates with your audience. From defining your unique selling points to structuring your pitch in a compelling narrative, you will learn how to captivate your networking connections and leave a lasting impact.

By honing your elevator pitch, you will have a powerful tool to open doors to new opportunities, spark engaging conversations, and set the stage for meaningful connections. So, let's dive in and master crafting an unforgettable elevator pitch!

What Is an Elevator Pitch?

An elevator pitch is a highly effective and strategic tool to make a lasting impression. The introduction is brief and meticulously planned, with the ability to be completed in the 30 to 2-minute duration it takes to ride an elevator. This short yet impactful pitch should provide an engaging overview of who you are, what you do, and what you want to achieve. By incorporating key details and showcasing your unique value proposition, the elevator pitch becomes an opportunity to captivate your audience and leave a memorable mark.

Crafting Your Elevator Pitch

Here are some key components to consider when crafting an effective elevator pitch:

Introduction: *Hi there! I hope you're doing well. My name is [Your Name], and I am reaching out to introduce myself.*

Who You Are: *I have a diverse background in [mention relevant fields or industries]. I hold the position of [your current role] and have expertise in [mention specific areas of knowledge or skills].*

Value Proposition: *My ability to [highlight specific skills or qualities] sets me apart. I am passionate about [mention a particular field or problem] and thrive on finding innovative solutions. I can bring a unique perspective and help achieve [mention specific goals or outcomes].*

Objective: *My main goal is to connect and network with professionals in [mention specific industry or field]. I believe in* *the power of collaboration and would love to explore potential opportunities or discuss shared interests.*

Closing: *I would love to hear more about your work and experiences. Please reach out if you'd like to continue the conversation or if there's anything I can assist you with. I am looking forward to connecting soon!*

Example Elevator Pitch

Hello, my name is [Your Name]. I'm a [Your Major/Field] student at [Your University], specialising in [Your Area of Expertise]. As a dedicated learner, I have honed my skills in [Specific Skills or Techniques] and gained valuable experience through practical projects and internships.

I am genuinely passionate about [Your Interest or Skill] and am determined to impact this field significantly. My goal is to [Your Goal or Objective], and I am actively seeking opportunities to collaborate with industry professionals and experts.

I would love to connect with you and learn more about your experiences and insights in this field. Your valuable knowledge and guidance would significantly contribute to my growth and development. Let's exchange ideas and explore the possibilities of working together to achieve remarkable outcomes.

Tailoring Your Pitch

Your elevator pitch should be adaptable to different situations and audiences. Whether you're at a professional event, a job fair, or a casual gathering, it's important to have variations that cater to each setting. For professional events, you can emphasise your expertise and highlight relevant accomplishments. At job fairs, you can focus on your skills and how they align with the industry or role. And for casual gatherings, you can inject some personality and share anecdotes that showcase your passion. Regardless of the context, the key is to keep it concise, engaging, and relevant to make a lasting impression.

Practice Makes Perfect

The more you practice your elevator pitch, the more natural and confident you'll become in delivering it. You can review and refine your delivery by practising in front of a mirror, with a friend, or even recording yourself. It will help you fine-tune your pitch to sound conversational as if you're having a genuine conversation rather than delivering a rehearsed speech. Remember to focus on your body language, tone of voice, and facial expressions to create a lasting impression. The goal is to captivate your audience and leave them wanting to know more about your idea, product, or service. So, take the time to practice, polish, and perfect your elevator pitch, and watch how it becomes a powerful tool in your arsenal of communication skills.

Customising for Specific Goals

Your elevator pitch, a concise and impactful introduction, can be tailored to meet different networking objectives. Whether you're seeking potential clients, investors, or collaborators, the key is highlighting your unique value proposition, showcasing your expertise, and demonstrating how you can solve their needs. By crafting a compelling and personalised elevator pitch, you can make a lasting impression and open doors to exciting opportunities. To achieve different networking goals, you can tailor your elevator pitch:

Job Seekers: When presenting yourself to potential employers, you must showcase your skills and experiences and the unique value you can bring to their organisation. Highlight specific accomplishments and how they demonstrate your expertise in a particular field. Additionally, mention any relevant certifications or training that further validate your qualifications. By doing so, you can stand out as a valuable candidate who can make a significant impact.

Information Seekers: As someone seeking knowledge and insights from experienced professionals, you must convey your genuine curiosity and eagerness to learn. Please explain why you are interested in gaining information from them and how you believe their expertise can benefit your personal or professional growth. Please show your appreciation for their time and knowledge and express your willingness to actively listen and absorb the valuable insights they have to offer.

Entrepreneurs: When presenting your business idea, it's essential to communicate the unique value it brings to the market. Please explain how your thought fills a gap or solves a problem and highlight any competitive advantages or innovative features that set it apart. Additionally, express what you seek regarding partnerships or advice, whether specific expertise, funding opportunities, or strategic alliances. Providing these details will paint a clearer picture of your vision and attract potential collaborators who resonate with your goals.

Mentorship Seekers: When reaching out to individuals for mentorship, you must convey your genuine admiration and respect for their achievements and expertise. Please explain why you chose them as a potential mentor and highlight aspects of their career or accomplishments that inspire you. Clearly express your eagerness to learn from their experiences and insights and explain how you believe their guidance can contribute to your personal and professional development. You can increase the likelihood of forming a meaningful mentorship relationship by showing genuine interest and appreciation.

Making a Memorable Impression

To guarantee that your elevator pitch makes a lasting impact, consider these valuable suggestions:

Be Enthusiastic: Show genuine enthusiasm for your field and goals. Let your passion shine through as you share your excitement for what you do. It will captivate the listener and inspire them to believe in your vision.

Use Stories: Weave a brief, relevant story into your pitch to make it more engaging. Share a personal anecdote or a client success story that highlights the positive impact of your work. This storytelling approach will connect with the listener and make your pitch more memorable.

Be Unique: Highlight what makes you stand out and what makes your journey different. Emphasise your unique strengths, experiences, or innovative approaches that set you apart from others in your field. You will leave a lasting impression on the listener by showcasing your distinctiveness.

Keep It Concise: Don't overwhelm your listeners with excessive information. Focus on the essentials and communicate your key points clearly and succinctly. Being concise will keep the listener's attention and ensure your message gets across effectively.

This chapter of my book explored the significance of crafting compelling elevator pitches for students and graduates. To illustrate this, I reference three insightful articles that provide practical strategies and examples.

The first article, **"5 Elevator Pitch Examples for Students + Quick Tips"** by John McTale and published on Storydoc, offers practical tips and tailored examples for students to create engaging elevator pitches.

Next, Kristen McCormick's article on WordStream, **"13 (Really) Good Elevator Pitch Examples & Templates (+How to Write Yours)"** presents 13 compelling elevator pitch examples, along with templates to create personalised pitches that are short, interesting, and confident.

Lastly, there's the guide by Kurian M. Tharakan on StrategyPeak, titled **"The Best Elevator Pitch Examples, Templates, and Tactics"** This guide offers a versatile elevator pitch template, adaptable for various situations such as networking events and job interviews for students and graduates. It emphasises the importance of engaging the audience with a compelling big idea and story.

These articles provide valuable insights and practical guidance for students and graduates seeking to create memorable elevator pitches for professional connections. By incorporating these examples and strategies, I wanted to emphasise the importance of elevator pitch to excess networking.

In the next chapter, we'll concentrate on the art of small talk and conversation, exploring the nuances and techniques essential for building connections and fostering meaningful relationships. This skill becomes particularly crucial after your elevator pitch has made a positive first impression. An effective elevator pitch sets the stage for engaging and productive networking interactions, allowing you to confidently introduce yourself, articulate your goals, and initiate lasting conversations. So, take the time to craft and refine your pitch, ensuring that it captures your unique qualities and aspirations compellingly and memorably.

The Art of Small Talk and Conversation

Your elevator pitch is your foot in the door, laying the foundation for meaningful connections. However, the true networking magic unfolds during the follow-up conversation. Bridges are built in these moments of small talk, effortlessly connecting you with others and transforming casual introductions into lasting connections. In this chapter, we will understand the art of small talk, exploring techniques to engage in productive conversations and create valuable relationships that can propel your personal and professional growth.

The Power of Small Talk

Small talk serves several critical networking functions, crucial in establishing meaningful connections. Firstly, it helps break the ice, creating a comfortable atmosphere for you and your networking partner to engage in conversation. By starting with light and casual topics, you can ease into deeper discussions more smoothly.

Moreover, small talk acts as a gateway to discovering common ground. It allows you to explore shared interests, experiences, or goals, laying the foundation for a stronger connection. Finding a topic of interest that resonates with both parties creates a sense of camaraderie. It facilitates a more fruitful exchange of ideas.

Beyond establishing commonalities, small talk is instrumental in building rapport. A friendly and engaging conversation fosters a sense of trust and familiarity, making it easier for individuals to connect personally. This connection can lead to long-lasting professional relationships, as people are more inclined to collaborate and support those they feel a connection with.

Lastly, small talk serves as a bridge to deeper conversations. It acts as a stepping stone, gradually paving the way for more substantial discussions and collaborations. By establishing rapport through small talk, individuals are likelier to open up and delve into more meaningful topics, sharing insights and experiences that can lead to valuable insights or partnerships.

In summary, small talk is not merely idle chatter but a strategic tool for effective networking. It helps break down barriers, uncovers commonalities, builds rapport, and facilitates deeper conversations, ultimately fostering connections that can propel personal and professional growth.

Keys to Effective Small Talk

Now that we understand the power of small talk, let's look into some essential keys to mastering this skill. Here are a few techniques that can help you engage in practical small discussions and build lasting connections:

Active Listening: The Key to Good Small Talk

The foundation of good small talk lies in active listening, a skill that enhances communication and deepens connections. To practice active listening, you should pay close attention to what the other person is saying, and demonstrate your interest by asking thoughtful follow-up questions. Set aside any distractions and avoid the temptation to plan your response while they are speaking. Instead, immerse yourself in the conversation, fostering a genuine connection and making the interaction more meaningful. By devoting your full attention to the present moment, you can genuinely engage in enriching small talk experiences.

Open-Ended Questions

Open-ended questions are a great way to spark meaningful conversations and explore deeper into someone's thoughts and experiences. By avoiding simple yes/no inquiries, you create an opportunity for the other person to share more about themselves and express their opinions. Start your questions with words like "what," "why," "how," or "tell me about..." to encourage a more elaborate and insightful response. This approach fosters a richer and more engaging conversation, allowing you to connect with others on a deeper level and better understand their perspectives and experiences. So, next time you want to ignite a meaningful discussion, remember the power of open-ended questions!

Shared Interests

One effective way to establish a genuine rapport in a conversation is by identifying and discussing common interests. These shared interests include hobbies, such as playing an instrument or hiking, favourite books or genres, like science fiction or self-help, or even industry-related topics, such as emerging trends or innovative technologies. You should try to create a natural flow in the conversation and foster a deeper connection with the other person by digging into these issues.

Positive Body Language

Mastering the art of non-verbal communication is crucial, as it can be just as impactful as the words you speak. One key aspect is maintaining steady eye contact, which shows attentiveness and builds trust and connection with others. Additionally, offering a warm and genuine smile can instantly create a welcoming and friendly atmosphere, making others feel comfortable in your presence. Lastly, adopting open body language, such as uncrossed arms and facing towards the person you're communicating with, signifies your engagement and approachability, encouraging others to feel more at ease and open to conversation. These small yet powerful gestures can enhance your interpersonal interactions and leave a positive impression on those around you.

Appropriate Topics

Focusing on safe topics that foster a positive and inclusive environment is highly recommended in professional settings. These topics include discussing recent industry news, sharing insights about the event you are attending, or engaging in conversations about everyday career-related experiences. By avoiding sensitive or controversial subjects, you can ensure a respectful and harmonious atmosphere conducive to productive interactions and professional growth.

Building Deeper Connections

Employing the following strategies and techniques to transition from casual chit-chat to forging more profound and meaningful connections is beneficial. By implementing these approaches, you can create a genuine and authentic atmosphere that fosters open communication, trust, and understanding, laying the foundation for more profound connections and relationships:

Share Your Experiences: One effective way to contribute to the discussion is by sharing personal anecdotes and insights related to the topic. By sharing your own experiences, you can provide valuable perspectives and engage others in a meaningful way.

Express Appreciation: Expressing gratitude is another critical aspect of effective communication. If someone shares valuable advice or information, take a moment to express your appreciation. In addition to encouraging more cooperation and knowledge exchange, this demonstrates respect for their input.

Find Opportunities for Collaboration: As conversations progress, it's common to discover shared goals or interests. When this happens, you should explore any collaborations possible. Examples could be working on a project together, sharing resources, or exchanging ideas and insights. Collaboration can lead to innovative solutions and more robust connections within the community.

Ask About Their Experiences: Active listening and genuine interest in others can significantly enhance the quality of conversations. Take your time to ask about the other person's experiences and journey. Fostering a deeper connection and understanding demonstrates your value for their input.

Follow-Up: After a conversation, it's essential to follow up to solidify the connection and express your enjoyment of the interaction. A follow-up message reinforces the positive impression and demonstrates your interest in staying connected. This may result from future partnerships, friendships, and chances for development and education.

Navigating Awkward Moments

Only some conversations will be smooth sailing. Awkward moments can happen unexpectedly, catching us off guard and leaving us momentarily at a loss for words. However, it is essential to remember that how we handle these awkward moments can make all the difference. Taking a deep breath, maintaining a calm demeanour, and responding gracefully and empathetically can help turn an uncomfortable situation into an opportunity for growth and understanding. So, view unpleasant situations as learning opportunities and enhancing your communication abilities.

Graceful Exits: In a conversation that isn't going well, it's crucial to exit while gracefully maintaining a positive and respectful tone. One way to do this is by expressing your intention to meet other attendees or engage in other activities. Doing so allows you to gracefully transition out of the conversation without causing any discomfort.

Recovery: We all make mistakes or say something awkward occasionally, and it's essential to acknowledge them with humour and move on. We're all human, and people appreciate authenticity. When you can laugh at yourself and accept your imperfections, it creates a sense of relatability and helps to diffuse any potential awkwardness. So, if you find yourself in a situation where you've made a mistake or said something awkward, take a moment to acknowledge it, add a touch of humour, and then gracefully move on to another topic.

Redirecting: Sometimes, conversations can take an uncomfortable turn or touch upon sensitive topics. In such situations, redirecting the conversation toward a neutral and non-controversial topic is helpful. By doing so, you can steer the conversation away from uncomfortable territory and create a more pleasant and inclusive atmosphere for everyone involved. The goal is to keep the discussion enjoyable and respectful for all participants.

Practice Makes Perfect

Small talk is an essential skill which can be honed with practice and experience. One effective way to hone this skill is by attending networking events, joining clubs, or conversing with classmates and colleagues. These activities help build your confidence and enhance your minor talk abilities.

In the following chapter, we will examine the power of LinkedIn and online networking. I will provide you with practical strategies to leverage digital connections for your professional growth, enabling you to expand your network and create valuable opportunities. However, for now, it is essential to remember that small talk serves as the bridge that connects you with others. By mastering the art of small conversation, you can establish lasting connections and open doors to many valuable opportunities. So, embrace the art of small talk and watch as it opens new horizons for your personal and professional growth.

The Power of LinkedIn and Online Networking

In today's fast-paced and interconnected digital age, online networking has become an indispensable and powerful tool for building and nurturing professional connections. With the rise of platforms like LinkedIn, professionals now have a centralised hub to showcase their skills, expertise, and personal brand to a global audience.

LinkedIn has emerged as the leading platform for connecting with like-minded professionals and establishing meaningful relationships in the professional world. It provides a unique space where individuals can connect with colleagues and peers, discover new opportunities, stay updated with industry trends, and engage in thought-provoking discussions.

In this chapter, we'll look at the incredible power of LinkedIn and online networking and the wide range of tools and services available to help you maximise your digital presence. I will also equip you with practical strategies to craft a compelling profile, engage with your network, and leverage the platform's tools to expand your professional reach.

By harnessing the power of online networking, you may establish yourself as a significant and influential participant in your field, opening the door to new collaborations, career improvements, and vital contacts with professionals who share your interests and goals. So, let's plunge into the exciting world of LinkedIn and discover the limitless opportunities it provides for professional growth and achievement.

The Significance of LinkedIn

LinkedIn is not just a social media platform but a professional networking hub connecting individuals from various industries worldwide. With its advanced features and capabilities, such as personalised job recommendations, industry insights, and professional development resources, LinkedIn has become an indispensable tool for students looking to expand their professional network and unlock exciting career opportunities. Whether connecting with industry experts, joining relevant groups, or showcasing your skills and experiences, LinkedIn provides a comprehensive platform for students to navigate the professional landscape and take proactive steps towards their future success.

Profile Showcase: LinkedIn provides an exceptional online platform for you to showcase your unique set of skills, valuable experiences, notable educational background, and impressive accomplishments. Whether you are a seasoned professional or just starting your career, LinkedIn offers a comprehensive space to highlight your professional journey and stand out.

Global Reach: With millions of users across the globe, LinkedIn offers an extensive and diverse network of professionals from various industries. This global reach allows you to connect with like-minded individuals, expand your professional network, and explore new opportunities on a worldwide scale. By engaging with professionals from different backgrounds, you can gain valuable insights, exchange ideas, and foster meaningful connections to propel your career forward.

Job Opportunities: LinkedIn has become a go-to platform for many companies and recruiters seeking talented individuals in today's competitive job market. By leveraging the power of LinkedIn, you can increase your visibility and attract potential employers who actively use the platform to find candidates for job openings and internships. With the ability to showcase your skills, experiences, and accomplishments, you can position yourself as a top candidate and seize exciting job opportunities that align with your career goals.

Industry Insights: LinkedIn offers a wealth of industry insights to keep you well-informed and up to date on your field's latest trends, news, and discussions. By following influential industry leaders and joining relevant groups, you can access valuable resources, thought-provoking content, and engaging discussions that can deepen your understanding of your industry. This practical knowledge can help you stay ahead of the curve, make informed decisions, and position yourself as a thought leader in your field.

Recommendations and Endorsements: One of the unique features of LinkedIn is the ability for your connections to endorse your skills and provide guidance. These endorsements and recommendations are potent testimonials that add credibility and authenticity to your profile. When potential employers or clients visit your profile, they can see firsthand the positive feedback from colleagues, mentors, and clients, which can strengthen your professional reputation and increase your chances of securing new opportunities.

Optimising Your LinkedIn Profile

To fully leverage the power of LinkedIn, it is crucial to create and maintain a strong profile that showcases your professional expertise and personal brand. Here are some key elements to consider:

Professional Photo: Choose a high-quality, professional-looking photo that reflects your personality and conveys a sense of credibility and approachability. Make sure your face is clear and visible.

Compelling Headline: Your headline should go beyond just stating your job title. Craft a compelling headline that succinctly captures your unique value proposition and highlights your essential skills or areas of expertise. Potential connections will notice this and become interested in learning more about you.

Summary: Your summary section lets you tell your professional story and make a strong impression. Use it to highlight your skills, experiences, and achievements, as well as your career goals and passions. Be concise yet engaging and consider including any notable accomplishments or projects that demonstrate your expertise.

Detailed Experience: You should provide detailed information about your education, work experience, projects, and relevant awards or honours. Use bullet points or paragraphs to highlight your responsibilities, accomplishments, and key outcomes in each role. Visitors will gain a better understanding of your professional journey and expertise as a result of this.

Skills and Endorsements:

You should list your core skills and encourage connections to endorse them. Be strategic and choose skills that align with your career goals and areas of expertise. Regularly update your skills to reflect and keep your evolving professional interests relevant.

Connections: Connect with classmates, professors, colleagues, and industry professionals to expand your network. Networking is a valuable aspect of LinkedIn, so actively seek out connections who share similar professional interests or can provide valuable insights and opportunities.

Recommendations: You should request recommendations from professors, supervisors, or colleagues who can vouch for your skills, work ethic, and professional achievements. Recommendations add credibility to your profile and can help showcase your abilities to potential employers or clients.

By paying attention to these details and consistently updating and optimising your profile, you can establish your professional presence on LinkedIn and make a lasting impression on your network and potential opportunities.

Building an Online Network

Building meaningful and relevant LinkedIn connections is crucial to achieving your goals. Here are some effective strategies to help you cultivate a valuable online network.

Connect with Purpose: When reaching out to potential connections, take the time to personalise your requests. Explain why you want to connect and how you believe the relationship can be mutually beneficial. This personal touch shows that you value their expertise and are genuinely interested in establishing a meaningful connection.

Join Industry Groups: LinkedIn groups offer a fantastic opportunity to engage in discussions and connect with like-minded professionals in your industry. By actively participating in these groups, you can expand your network, gain insights from others, and foster valuable relationships with individuals who share your interests and goals.

Follow Industry Leaders: Identify influential professionals and thought leaders in your field and follow their LinkedIn profiles. Doing so lets you stay updated on industry trends, news, and insights. Knowing what these leaders are doing and saying can provide you with inspiration and valuable knowledge to enhance your professional journey.

Participate Actively: Actively engaging with your connections is critical to nurturing relationships. Take the time to comment on their posts, share your insights, and help when it is relevant. By actively participating in conversations, you demonstrate your expertise, build rapport, and contribute to the growth and engagement of your network.

Share Valuable Content: Sharing valuable content is a great way to establish yourself as a knowledgeable contributor and add value to your network. Whether it's sharing industry articles, research findings, or your thoughts on relevant topics, providing valuable content showcases your expertise and encourages meaningful interactions with your connections.

Through LinkedIn, you can build a robust and valuable online network that supports your professional growth and opens doors to new opportunities. The idea is to cultivate and nurture your LinkedIn connections deliberately, authentically, and proactively.

The Art of Online Etiquette

Maintaining professionalism on LinkedIn is essential for creating a positive online presence. There are several critical practices to remember to achieve this.

Be Respectful: Remember to always treat others with courtesy and respect when you're online. It's important to create a positive and friendly environment for everyone. Avoiding harassment and using derogatory language is part of this. By fostering a culture of respect, you contribute to a supportive and inclusive professional community.

Share Value: When posting on LinkedIn, aim to provide value to your connections. Sharing educational articles, perspectives, and firsthand accounts about your field or business can help achieve this. Doing so positions yourself as a valuable resource and establishes yourself as a thought leader in your area.

Engage Thoughtfully: If you join discussions or respond to comments, do so thoughtfully and constructively. Avoid engaging in arguments or making derogatory remarks. Instead, contribute to the conversation by providing thoughtful insights, asking questions, and offering helpful suggestions. Your professional network will benefit from these deep and fruitful conversations.

Avoid Oversharing: While it's great to share your professional journey and accomplishments, finding the right balance and avoiding oversharing personal information is really important. Maintain a professional tone and focus on sharing relevant and insightful content that aligns with your career goals. By doing this, you can preserve boundaries and keep the focus of your LinkedIn profile on your professional brand.

By adhering to these guidelines, you will create a professional and strong online presence on LinkedIn. This will increase your networking chances and allow you to showcase your expertise to a larger audience.

Networking Beyond LinkedIn

While LinkedIn is undoubtedly a powerful platform for online networking, it's essential to focus on something other than this avenue. Use social media platforms like X(Twitter), Instagram, or Facebook to maximise your digital presence. Creating and maintaining a blog or website can give you even more opportunities to showcase your expertise, connect with a broader audience, and establish yourself as a thought leader. By diversifying your online presence, you can amplify your professional reach and broaden your network beyond the confines of a single platform.

In the upcoming chapter, we will talk about the fascinating world of informational interviews and mentorship. These invaluable tools can be pivotal in your networking journey, offering unique insights and guidance from experienced professionals. By leveraging the power of LinkedIn and engaging in online networking, you can broaden your horizons, expand your connections, and forge meaningful relationships with like-minded individuals who align with your passions and aspirations. Together, we will explore the limitless possibilities that await you on this exciting path of personal and professional growth.

Informational Interviews and Mentorship

One of the most influential and rewarding ways to expand your professional network, gain valuable insights, and accelerate your career growth is through the power of informational interviews and mentorship. These intentional and purposeful interactions provide a unique opportunity to connect with experienced professionals in your field, tap into their wisdom, and glean practical advice to propel you forward.

During informational interviews, you can learn firsthand from individuals who have walked the path you aspire to tread. They can share their experiences, offer industry-specific knowledge, and provide valuable insights into current trends and best practices. By actively listening and engaging in thoughtful conversations, you can uncover new opportunities, refine your career goals, and gain a broader perspective on your chosen field.

Conversely, mentorship goes beyond just gathering information - it involves building a long-term relationship with a trusted guide who can provide support, encouragement, and guidance throughout your professional journey. A mentor can give personalised advice tailored to your unique circumstances, help you navigate challenges, and offer valuable feedback on your career development. They can also share their network and connections, opening doors to new opportunities and expanding your reach within your industry.

In this chapter, we'll look at the art of informational interviews and the transforming power of mentorship. By utilising these vital resources, you may accelerate your professional development, build significant connections, and open new opportunities for success.

Informational Interviews: What Are They?

Informational interviews are highly beneficial and structured conversations with professionals with expertise in your field. Unlike job interviews, these interviews serve as opportunities to gain valuable insights, advice, and information about a specific industry or role. You can expand your knowledge, establish valuable connections, and enhance your networking capabilities by conducting informational interviews. As a result, they are an invaluable resource, particularly for students interested in exploring potential career paths and broadening their horizons.

The Benefits of Informational Interviews

Informational interviews offer several key advantages that can significantly benefit your career exploration and development:

Learning Opportunity: Through these interviews, you could gather in-depth information about a specific field, industry, or role that may not be readily available online or in books. You can gain valuable insights, insider knowledge, and practical advice from professionals already working in the field.

Networking: In addition to gathering information, informational interviews also provide a platform for you to build meaningful connections with professionals in your desired field. These connections can offer guidance, mentorship, and potential referrals, significantly enhancing your career prospects.

Career Clarity: One of the significant benefits of conducting informational interviews is gaining clarity about your career goals. By engaging in conversations with professionals with firsthand experience, you can better understand the skills, qualifications, and experiences required for your chosen path. This clarity can help you make informed decisions and take purposeful steps towards your desired career.

Hidden Opportunities: Informational interviews can also reveal remote job opportunities or unannounced internships, which is an additional benefit. Professionals you connect with may have insider knowledge about upcoming opportunities or be aware of vacancies within their networks, giving you an edge in your job search.

Personal Growth: Engaging in these conversations expands your professional network and contributes to your personal growth. By actively listening, asking thoughtful questions, and effectively communicating your interests and aspirations, you can enhance your communication and networking skills, which are valuable assets in any career.

Overall, informational interviews provide a unique and valuable opportunity to gain knowledge, build connections, clarify your career goals, uncover hidden opportunities, and foster personal growth. Consider incorporating them into your career exploration strategy to maximise your success chances.

How to Conduct Informational Interviews?

Informational interviews are a powerful tool for gathering insights about a specific industry, company, or role from someone with firsthand experience. They provide an opportunity to ask questions that can't be answered by reading an article or browsing a company's website. They also create a chance to build valuable connections in your field of interest. Here are some essential steps to follow when conducting an informational interview:

Identify Potential Contacts: First, explore various platforms such as LinkedIn, industry events, or alumni networks to find professionals in your field. Take the time to research and identify individuals who align with your interests and goals.

Reach Out: Next, craft a concise email introducing yourself and expressing your genuine interest in their work. Explain why you are reaching out and kindly request a brief meeting or conversation to discuss their experiences and insights.

Prepare Thoughtful Questions

Before the interview, take the opportunity to develop a list of well-thought-out questions.

You might want to ask about their career path, any lessons they've learned, challenges they've faced, and their thoughts on the future of the industry. It's always interesting to hear about someone's journey and gain insights from their experiences.

Tailor your questions to showcase your interest and willingness to learn from their expertise.

Conduct the Interview: Don't forget to show respect for the interviewee's time during the interview. Start by expressing gratitude for their willingness to share their knowledge. Ask your prepared questions attentively and actively listen to their responses. Take notes and engage in meaningful conversations to gain valuable insights.

Express Gratitude: Don't forget to send a thank-you note after the interview! It's a great way to show your appreciation. Thank them for their time, insights, and willingness to share their experiences. Personalise the message to highlight specific points from the discussion that resonated with you.

Follow Up and Nurture the Connection: To keep the connection going, make sure to reach out to the interviewee from time to time with updates on your progress. It's like checking in with a friend, letting them know how things are coming along. It's all about staying in touch and keeping them in the loop. Share any milestones or achievements that may interest them. Doing this lets you retain their interest and help you develop your relationship.

Conducting informational interviews can be a great approach to learn new things and broaden your professional network. You may take advantage of these possibilities and develop valuable contacts in your field by following these steps.

The Importance of Mentorship

A mentor is an experienced professional who can provide invaluable guidance, support, and advice as you navigate your educational and career journey.

Having a mentor by your side helps you gain insights and perspectives from their wealth of experience and opens doors to opportunities you may not have otherwise discovered. Mentorship relationships foster personal and professional growth by offering a safe learning, collaboration, and continuous development space. Embrace the power of mentorship and unlock your full potential!

Finding a Mentor

Finding a mentor as a student can be an enriching experience that significantly contributes to your academic and personal growth. A mentor often has experience and knowledge in areas you're interested in and can provide guidance, advice, and support as you navigate your educational journey.

Mentors can come in many forms. They could be teachers, professors, professionals in your field of interest, or even upper-level students. They are individuals who have walked the path you're embarking on and can provide insights that textbooks and lectures may need to cover.

The benefits of having a mentor are significant. They can help you understand complex concepts, offer advice for career paths, provide networking opportunities, and give constructive feedback to help you improve. They can also provide emotional support and encouragement during challenging times. Here are some steps to help you in the process:

Seek Compatibility: Look for a mentor whose experiences, values, and career path align with your goals and interests. Consider what specific skills or knowledge you hope to gain from a mentor and how their expertise can support your professional growth.

Leverage Your Network: Reach out to professors, colleagues, or professionals you've met to ask for recommendations or introductions to potential mentors. Tell them about your aspirations and what you seek in a mentor. They may have valuable insights or connections to help you find the right fit.

Online Platforms: Use websites like LinkedIn and mentoring-specific platforms that can connect you with potential mentors. Create a compelling profile highlighting your background, interests, and goals.

Make it a point to actively connect and engage with relevant communities and groups. This will help you expand your network and increase your chances of finding a mentor who suits your needs. Trust me, it's a game-changer!

Finding a mentor goes beyond just seeking advice - it's about building a genuine connection. So, be proactive, adaptable, and open to new ideas.

Establishing a Mentorship Relationship

Once you've identified a potential mentor as a student, it's crucial to approach the relationship thoughtfully. It involves considering how the mentorship fits your academic goals, preparing for initial contact, and cultivating a mutually beneficial relationship. Here are some additional details to consider:

Requesting Mentorship: When reaching out to a potential mentor, it is essential to craft a polite and well-thought-out email or message. Clearly explain your goals and aspirations, emphasising why you believe their guidance would be valuable to you. Express your genuine interest in being mentored by them.

Setting Expectations: Understanding what you hope to gain from the mentorship is essential. Take the time to outline your specific objectives and the commitment level you seek. By clearly communicating your expectations, you and your mentor will have a solid foundation for the mentorship journey.

Respecting Their Time: Keep in mind that your mentor is probably a busy person with a lot on their plate. Please respect their time by being punctual and prepared for each interaction. Before every meeting or conversation, ensure you have done your homework and come equipped with specific questions or topics to discuss. It demonstrates your commitment to the mentorship and provides fruitful interaction.

Regular Communication: Regularly communicating with your mentor is critical to a successful mentorship. Schedule regular check-ins or meetings to discuss progress, challenges, and new insights. Keep your mentor updated on your achievements and any milestones you have reached. Showing appreciation for their guidance and informing them will strengthen the mentorship bond.

Two-Way Learning: Remember, mentorship is not just a one-way street. It should be a mutually beneficial relationship where both parties can learn and grow. While your mentor provides guidance and expertise, be open to sharing your knowledge and experiences. Embrace the opportunity to contribute to the relationship by offering insights or perspectives that may also be valuable to your mentor.

You may develop a meaningful and effective mentorship connection by following these recommendations and adding more detail to your approach.

Informational interviews and mentorship can profoundly impact your professional network, knowledge acquisition, and personal growth. These invaluable connections are about seeking advice or referrals and nurturing relationships that can last a lifetime. The next chapter is all about navigating the job search effectively through strategic networking. However, it is crucial to remember that proactively reaching out to experienced professionals and establishing meaningful mentorship relationships can provide invaluable guidance, unwavering support, and a robust network to rely on as you progress in your academic and professional endeavours. These connections can offer insights, opportunities, and a sense of belonging that will significantly contribute to your success and fulfilment.

Navigating the Job Search Through Networking

As a student, building a solid professional network can be an invaluable asset that can open doors to exciting job opportunities and pave the way for a successful career launch. In this insightful chapter, we will look into the art of skilfully navigating the job search process through the power of networking. I will provide you with a comprehensive array of strategies and techniques to help you effectively leverage your connections and transform them into promising job leads, giving you a competitive edge in the competitive job market.

The Importance of Networking in the Job Search

Networking is a crucial aspect of the job search, especially for students preparing to enter the workforce. It involves building and maintaining professional relationships that can provide support, advice, and opportunities.

In your job search, networking can be a powerful tool. It allows you to connect with individuals and organisations within your desired industry. It's not just about who you know but also who knows you. The more connections you have, the greater your visibility and chances of landing the right opportunity. Here's why networking is so important during the job search:

Hidden Opportunities: In the vast job market, many opportunities remain hidden from the public eye. Networking is a secret gateway, granting you access to these unadvertised positions. Connecting with professionals in your field increases your chances of discovering these hidden gems that could be the perfect fit for your career.

Referrals: Referrals can make all the difference when you stand out in a sea of job applications. Networking allows you to tap into the power of personal connections. When someone from your network refers you for a job, it adds a layer of credibility and trust to your application. Employers are more likely to take notice and give your application the attention it deserves.

Insider Insights: One of the most valuable aspects of networking is gaining insider insights from experienced professionals. By connecting with those who have already navigated the industry, you can learn firsthand about company cultures, industry trends, and even the hiring process. These insights provide a competitive edge, helping you tailor your job search strategy and make informed decisions.

Personal Support: Job hunting can be an emotionally challenging journey. Here's where your support system comes in to offer priceless emotional assistance. They understand the highs and lows of the job search process. They can provide guidance, encouragement, and motivation along the way. Their support can help you stay focused, maintain a positive mindset, and navigate any obstacles that come your way.

So, consider the power of networking in your job search. It's not just about exchanging business cards or making connections; it's about building relationships that can open doors to hidden opportunities, enhance your application, provide insider insights, and offer the support you need to succeed.

Effective Job Search Networking Strategies

Here are some effective strategies to maximise the power of your professional network during your job search. By leveraging the connections, you have cultivated over time, you can tap into a wealth of opportunities and resources that can significantly enhance your chances of finding the perfect job. Whether attending industry events, reaching out to mentors and colleagues, or actively engaging in online communities, proactively leveraging your network can open doors and provide valuable insights and support throughout your job search journey. So, take advantage of the power of networking and unlock new possibilities for your career success. Here are some additional tips: -

Leverage Your LinkedIn Network

Your LinkedIn profile is essentially your online resume, and it's one of the first things recruiters see when looking for potential candidates. Regularly updating your profile shows that you're active on the platform and allows you to tailor your profile to reflect your current job interests and career goals.

Sharing relevant content on LinkedIn helps demonstrate your knowledge and engagement in your industry. Jobs that could assist people in your network, thought-provoking articles that offer insightful viewpoints, or updates on the most recent events in your field can all be examples.

LinkedIn offers a robust job search feature that allows you to discover various job opportunities. You can filter these job postings by multiple criteria, including location, industry, and experience level.

LinkedIn is a powerful tool for networking. Use it to reach out to professionals in your field of interest. You can ask for advice, gain insights about the industry, or even request informational interviews.

Attend Networking Events

You should attend job fairs, industry-specific conferences, and alumni events. These are great opportunities to meet potential employers and make valuable in-person connections. These events provide an excellent opportunity to network with professionals in your field and learn about industry trends.

Before attending, take the time to prepare and bring multiple copies of your resume and business cards to distribute. You can easily share your qualifications and contact information with potential employers and other professionals.

following up with the connections you made is crucial after the event. Send personalised emails or connect with them on LinkedIn to express your continued interest in their company or industry. In addition to demonstrating your excitement for future opportunities, this helps keep the connection going.

Utilise Alumni Networks

Your school alums can provide valuable insights and job leads to enhance your career prospects significantly. Their firsthand experience and industry knowledge can offer unique perspectives and guidance.

Attending alum events, actively seeking out your alum association, and connecting with fellow graduates on

LinkedIn are all highly recommended ways to take advantage of this invaluable network.

By doing so, you can establish meaningful connections, expand your professional network, and access many opportunities that may not be available elsewhere.

Informational Interviews

You should conduct informational interviews with professionals in your desired field. This will help you gain valuable insights and expand your network. The result entails contacting experts in your target industry and setting up meetings to learn from their experiences and perspectives.

Express your job search goals and aspirations during these interviews, and kindly ask if they have any leads, recommendations, or contacts that could help you in your quest for the perfect job opportunity. By doing so, you can tap into their network and increase your chances of finding relevant job openings or getting referred to potential employers. Building meaningful connections and seeking professional guidance can significantly enhance your job search journey.

Be Clear About Your Goals

When contacting your network for job assistance, you must communicate the type of role you seek, your relevant skills, and what makes you a good fit.

Providing specific details about your experience and qualifications can help your network better understand how they can assist you in your job search.

Additionally, explaining why you believe those individuals can benefit your search is helpful when requesting introductions to people who can help you achieve your job search goals. Highlighting shared connections, industry expertise, or relevant experience can increase the likelihood of receiving valuable introductions.

Volunteer and Intern

Volunteering or interning in your chosen field can be an incredibly effective way to expand your professional network while gaining invaluable hands-on experience. By immersing yourself in real-world situations, you enhance your skills and establish meaningful connections with like-minded individuals who share your passion and ambition.

Another strategy to consider is helping with ongoing projects within your organisation. By proactively seeking opportunities to contribute, you demonstrate your dedication and eagerness to learn and have the chance to collaborate with experienced colleagues. This collaborative environment fosters knowledge sharing and allows you to learn from their expertise, ultimately enhancing your professional growth and expanding your network within the organisation.

Online Professional Groups

You should also join online professional groups on platforms like LinkedIn or specialized industry forums. These groups provide an excellent opportunity to connect with like-minded professionals, expand your network, and stay updated on your field's latest trends and developments. You can engage in meaningful discussions, share valuable insights, and seek advice from experienced professionals.

Participate actively in group discussions by asking thought-provoking questions and contributing your expertise. The following demonstrates your knowledge and enthusiasm for your field while also assisting you in establishing yourself as a valuable community member.

You can build relationships, gain visibility, and discover new career opportunities by actively engaging with others.

To achieve successful engagement, be proactive and consistent. Allocate time each week to interact with the group, contribute excellent material, and establish yourself as a trusted professional in your field.

Follow-Up and Gratitude

After you have leveraged your professional network to uncover job opportunities, it is of utmost importance to show your appreciation and maintain strong connections:

Send a heartfelt thank-you email to everyone offering assistance or referrals. Personalise your message by highlighting how their support has been invaluable to you.

Stay in touch with your network by regularly updating them on your progress. Tell them about any interviews, job offers, or career advancements you have achieved. Express your sincere gratitude for their ongoing support and guidance.

Share your success stories with your network to reinforce the value of your professional connections. Whether it is landing a dream job, securing an important interview, or making significant strides in your career, let your network celebrate these milestones with you. Showing off your accomplishments and fortifying your relationships with your connections are two things it does.

By taking these actions, you will express your thanks, and cultivate and expand your professional connections, laying the groundwork for future partnerships and possibilities.

Networking is a continuous activity rather than a one-time effort. Long-term success requires the development and maintenance of professional connections. Even after you've secured a job, continue nurturing your relationships by staying in touch, offering support, and seeking opportunities to collaborate. These connections can be vital to your career growth and advancement, opening doors to new possibilities, mentorship, and valuable insights. So, prioritise networking and invest time and effort into cultivating meaningful connections that can propel your professional journey forward.

As we conclude this chapter, we evaluated the power of networking and its impact on navigating the job search. Here are my recommendations on further reading into three insightful case studies that shed light on the importance of building solid connections and leveraging them to uncover job opportunities.

The first case study, **"How to Land A Job Through Networking"** was written by Wasim Hajjiri, a renowned author and executive career coach. Hajjiri provides practical advice on job hunting through networking, emphasising that this method secures approximately 80% of jobs. He stresses the need to dedicate significant time to networking and employ various strategies to enhance the chances of receiving job offers.

Also, the case study **"5 Tips for Networking Your Way to a Job on LinkedIn"**, published on SUCCESS, focuses on leveraging LinkedIn for job search purposes. It emphasises the significance of being active on the platform and making one's profile visible to recruiters. By following these tips, job seekers can significantly enhance their chances of receiving job offers.

These case studies collectively underscore the vital role networking plays in the job search process. They offer practical strategies and valuable insights that can assist job seekers in building a solid network and leveraging it to uncover job opportunities.

In the following chapter, we'll examine the complexities of networking etiquette and the best practices for quickly navigating the professional world. This comprehensive guidance will equip you with the knowledge and skills to maintain professionalism throughout your networking journey, ensuring you make a lasting impression on potential connections. Networking goes beyond just making new contacts. It's like having a secret weapon that can unlock doors to amazing opportunities you might never find through regular job applications. Trust me, the power of networking can open up a whole new world of job possibilities for you.

Networking Etiquette and Best Practices

Maintaining professionalism and adhering to networking etiquette are paramount in the professional world. These practices help build and nurture your professional connections and contribute to your overall success. This comprehensive chapter aims to equip you with the guidelines and best practices to ensure that your networking interactions are respectful and highly effective, enabling you to forge meaningful and lasting connections that can propel your career forward.

Networking Etiquette

Networking is a powerful tool for career development and job hunting. Still, it's also a social process that requires tact, professionalism, and respect. Understanding networking etiquette can significantly affect how effectively you build and maintain professional relationships as a student. Here are some fundamental principles of networking etiquette:

Respect Others' Time

When scheduling meetings or follow-up conversations, it is of utmost importance to be punctual and respect the schedules of your contacts. It demonstrates professionalism and consideration for their valuable time.

Additionally, it is crucial to keep interactions concise and focused, ensuring that you respect their time commitments. Doing so creates an environment of efficiency and effectiveness, allowing for productive and meaningful discussions.

Be Polite and Courteous

Always maintain a polite and respectful tone in all forms of communication, including face-to-face interactions, email exchanges, and social media interactions. This helps foster positive relationships and avoid misunderstandings. Remember to use appropriate salutations and maintain a professional tone when communicating. Address others respectfully and courteously to set the foundation for effective communication and collaboration. Additionally, express gratitude for any assistance or advice received to demonstrate appreciation and acknowledge the contributions of others. This will strengthen relationships and encourage more cooperation and support.

Be Mindful of Personal Space

When participating in in-person networking events, it is crucial to be conscious of personal space and show respect for the boundaries of others. Remember to maintain an appropriate distance and avoid invading someone's personal space. Doing so creates a comfortable and respectful environment for everyone involved, fostering positive and meaningful connections.

When interacting with others, it's essential to maintain a comfortable distance and respect their personal space. By giving people the physical space, they need, we create an environment that promotes mutual respect and comfort in social interactions.

Don't Overwhelm Contacts

It is advisable for you to refrain from sending excessive messages or connection requests to the same person. Building a genuine connection requires a balanced approach, allowing for meaningful interactions and respecting the recipient's boundaries. A considerate and mindful approach can establish more fruitful and long-lasting relationships in your professional network.

It is essential to show patience and understanding if the person you are communicating with cannot respond immediately. Recognise that people have different schedules and responsibilities that may prevent them from responding immediately. By being patient and understanding, you create a positive and supportive environment that fosters effective communication. Everyone appreciates when others are considerate of their time and circumstances.

Best Practices

Networking can play a major role in your professional journey, opening doors to opportunities and relationships that can have a significant impact on your career. As you transition into the professional world, it's important to understand and practice good networking etiquette. Here are some key things to keep in mind:

Always Follow Up

After attending a networking event or engaging in a meaningful conversation, sending a thoughtful follow-up message is always a good practice to express your sincere appreciation for the interaction. It allows you to solidify the connection further and leaves a positive impression.

You can also use this opportunity to provide any updates or progress that may be relevant to the conversation. You can continue the conversation by sharing new developments or insights and demonstrate your commitment to building a mutually beneficial relationship. Effective communication and ongoing engagement are crucial to establishing lasting connections in professional settings.

Reciprocate

Networking is a two-way street that involves building mutually beneficial relationships. It's not just about what you can gain from your network but also about how you can contribute and help others. Be open to offering your support, guidance, and assistance whenever you have the opportunity to do so.

When engaging with others in your network, actively listen and understand their needs and challenges. Then, offer your valuable insights, experiences, and expertise when it's relevant and can truly benefit the other person. You can strengthen your network and foster long-lasting relationships by providing meaningful assistance and sharing knowledge.

Be Specific in Your Requests

When seeking advice, introductions, or referrals, you must be specific about what you're seeking. Whether it's guidance on a particular project, an introduction to a potential client, or a referral for a job opportunity, clearly stating your goals will make it easier for the contact to understand how they can help and increase the likelihood of a successful outcome.

Moreover, providing context or background information about your situation can help the contact better comprehend your needs and tailor their assistance accordingly. By sharing relevant details such as your industry, current challenges, or specific areas where you require support, you can engage in a more meaningful conversation and establish a stronger connection with the person you're contacting.

Maintain a Professional Online Presence

It is essential to regularly review your online presence, including your social media profiles, to ensure that they accurately portray a professional image. It involves limiting or eliminating content likely to be interpreted as impersonal and looking for out-of-date or unnecessary information.

Curating your online presence by including relevant and engaging content demonstrating your expertise and professionalism is also advisable.

Sharing industry news and insights, participating in professional discussions, and highlighting your accomplishments and skills are examples.

Stay Informed

To foster meaningful discussions with your professional network, stay informed about the latest industry news, emerging trends, and upcoming events. Demonstrate your knowledge and expertise by engaging in insightful conversations on current topics.

Additionally, don't hesitate to share your valuable insights and expertise with your connections whenever it aligns with the conversation. The opportunity to showcase your knowledge establishes your credibility and positions you as a thought leader in your field.

Be Adaptable

When navigating various networking situations, it's essential to consider that different scenarios may call for different approaches. Take the time to assess the context and the individuals you're interacting with and adapt your communication style accordingly. This level of adaptability ensures effective and meaningful connections.

In addition, it's crucial to remain flexible in your networking efforts. Embrace new experiences and seize opportunities that come your way. By being open-minded, you can expand your network, gain valuable insights, and unlock unforeseen possibilities that may lead to personal and professional growth.

Handling Rejection and Challenges

Not all networking interactions will be successful or lead to connections. It's important to remember that handling rejection or challenges is integral to the networking process.

Suppose someone declines your connection request or isn't interested in helping. In that case, respecting that person's decision and moving away is critical.

Don't take it personally; everyone has different priorities and preferences. Instead, focus on building relationships with those who are interested and willing to engage.

Furthermore, it's essential to learn from your networking experiences, even those that didn't go as planned. Reflect on what worked well and what could be improved. Doing so can enhance your networking skills and approach, making future interactions more fruitful.

Networking is a never-ending learning experience, and each one contributes to your overall growth and development. Accept the hurdles and utilise them to improve your networking skills.

Networking is a short-term and long-term investment in your professional growth and success. By consistently practising proper networking etiquette and following best practices, you can establish and nurture meaningful connections that have the potential to unlock valuable opportunities and contribute to your personal growth.

The following chapter of this guide will review the significance of continuous learning in networking. I will provide insightful strategies for evolving and adapting your networking approach throughout your career. It's essential to recognise that networking is a dynamic process, and your commitment to ongoing learning will play a crucial role in its long-term success and value. So, embrace the opportunity to expand your knowledge and skills, as it will undoubtedly enhance your networking capabilities and open doors to new horizons.

The Journey of Continuous Learning in Networking

Networking is not a static process but an ever-evolving journey that can lead to personal and professional growth. In this chapter, we'll discuss the value of continual learning in networking, highlighting the need to remain current with industry trends, broadening your knowledge base, and polishing new abilities. Throughout your career, you'll be better able to navigate the constantly shifting landscape and create lasting connections that can help you succeed if you consistently modify your networking strategies. Networking is about exchanging business cards and building genuine relationships that foster collaboration and open doors to new opportunities. As a result, enjoy the adventure of networking, embrace the power of lifelong learning, and maximise the potential of your professional network.

Networking as a Dynamic Process

Your professional network is not something you build once and forget about; it's a living, dynamic entity that requires continuous nurturing. As the world and industries evolve and as your goals and aspirations transform, it becomes even more crucial to engage in networking actively. By consistently expanding your connections, staying updated on industry trends, and fostering meaningful relationships, you can ensure that your network remains relevant, valuable, and a source of ongoing opportunities and growth. Embrace networking as a continuing process to unlock its full potential and maximise your professional success.

The Importance of Staying Informed

Staying informed in networking refers to keeping abreast of industry trends, news, and developments. It enhances conversations with potential connections for students, demonstrating a commitment to their field. Being informed helps identify opportunities like job openings or internships, prepares students for professional interactions, and builds credibility. Knowledge outside their main interest can also bridge conversational gaps, allowing connections with diverse individuals. Effective networking isn't just about who you know and what you know. By staying informed, students can become more effective networkers, opening doors to various opportunities.

Industry Trends: It is vital to continuously monitor and stay updated on changes and developments within your industry. You can stay ahead of the curve and maintain a competitive edge by staying informed about new technologies, best practices, and emerging trends.

Career Evolution: Your goals and aspirations will naturally evolve as you progress. It is vital to ensure that your network is aligned with your current objectives, as they can play a crucial role in supporting your career advancement and helping you achieve your goals.

Skill Development: Networking provides valuable connections and opens learning and skill development doors. You can enhance your professional growth and expand your capabilities by seeking mentors or contacts to help you acquire or refine new skills. This continuous focus on skill development will enable you to adapt to the evolving demands of your industry and stay ahead in your career journey.

Networking at Different Stages of Your Career

Your networking strategies will differ depending on where you are in your career journey. When starting, building a solid foundation is essential to attending industry events, connecting with professionals, and seeking mentorship opportunities. As you progress in your career, you can expand your network by joining professional associations, participating in conferences, and leveraging social media platforms. With each stage of your job, your networking approach should evolve to align with your goals and aspirations. Remember, networking is a continuous process that can open doors to new opportunities and professional growth.

As a student:

You should prioritize building a solid foundation network by connecting with your classmates, professors, and professionals in your field of interest. Engage in meaningful conversations, seek advice, and establish valuable relationships that can propel your career forward.

Take advantage of opportunities like attending career fairs, internships, and joining student organisations. These experiences provide invaluable early exposure to networking, allowing you to expand your professional connections and broaden your career horizons. Embrace these opportunities to learn, grow, and make a lasting impact in your chosen field.

Early Career:

Why not take the initiative to seek mentorship and set up some informational interviews with professionals from different careers and industries? Trust me, it'll give you some incredible insights and guidance as you navigate your career journey.

Additionally, make it a point to attend industry-specific events, conferences, and workshops. These gatherings offer opportunities to expand your knowledge and skills and help you build a network of like-minded professionals who can provide valuable advice and support in making informed career choices.

Embracing Change

It is critical to remain open and adaptable in your networking strategies to ensure long-term success in your career. Here are some essential tips to help you navigate this dynamic landscape:

Review your network periodically: Take the time to assess your connections and evaluate if they align with your current goals. You should consider trimming your network and focus on quality over quantity.

Seek out new mentors: Look for individuals who have achieved what you aspire to and can offer guidance and support. Building relationships with mentors can provide valuable insights and help you broaden your horizons.

Expand your horizons: Don't limit yourself to your immediate industry or profession. Explore networking opportunities in related fields or communities to gain fresh perspectives and uncover new opportunities.

Continue to learn and grow: You should invest in your personal and professional development. Attend conferences, workshops, or webinars to acquire new skills and stay current with industry trends. The more you expand your knowledge, the more valuable you become as a networker.

Adaptability is key. Embrace change and be open to new networking opportunities that come your way. By continuously refining your strategies and embracing growth, you'll position yourself for long-term success in your career.

Networking is not a one-time activity but an ongoing journey that can lead to significant personal and professional growth. As you navigate your career, it is crucial to continuously learn, stay well-informed, and adapt your networking strategies to meet your evolving goals and aspirations. By embracing networking as a dynamic and ever-evolving process, you can build and maintain meaningful connections with like-minded individuals who share your passions and drive. These connections can provide valuable insights, support, and opportunities that will propel you towards success and enable you to flourish in your chosen career path. So, continue to invest time and effort in nurturing these connections, attending industry events, participating in online communities, and seeking mentorship opportunities. Remember, networking is not just about exchanging business cards or making small talk; it is about building genuine relationships that can impact your professional journey.

Measuring the Impact of Your Networking Efforts

While networking is a dynamic and ever-changing process that involves building relationships and making connections, it is also crucial to measure the impact of your efforts. In this chapter, we will discuss the various methods and techniques to evaluate the effectiveness of your networking activities. By assessing the outcomes of your networking endeavours, you can identify areas for improvement, refine your strategies, and maximise the benefits derived from your professional connections.

Setting Clear Goals

To truly gauge the impact of your networking efforts, it's crucial to set clear and specific goals. These goals will help align your networking activities with your desired outcomes and make tracking your progress much more effective. By defining your goals, you can focus your efforts and evaluate the success of your networking endeavours more comprehensively:

Job Search: Are you currently seeking new job opportunities or looking to advance your career? Whether you are exploring job options in your field or considering a career transition, having clarity on your job search goals can help you focus your efforts and maximise your chances of success.

Information Gathering: If you are interested in gaining valuable insights and knowledge about your industry or field of interest, you should keep up with the latest trends, market developments, and industry news. This will provide you with a competitive edge and help you make informed decisions in your professional journey.

Skill Development: If you are looking to broaden your skill set and acquire new skills or knowledge, continuous learning and upskilling are crucial for your professional growth in today's fast-paced and rapidly evolving work environment. Whether you want to develop your technical skills or enhance your soft skills, investing in your personal and professional development can open up new opportunities and boost your career prospects.

Mentorship: Are you seeking guidance, support, and mentorship from experienced professionals? Finding a mentor or mentee can be immensely valuable in your career journey. A mentor can provide practical advice, share their expertise, and help you navigate challenges and obstacles. Likewise, being a mentor to someone can be a rewarding experience where you can share your knowledge and contribute to someone else's growth and development.

Business Opportunities: If you are interested, you can explore partnership opportunities, collaborations, or entrepreneurial endeavors. Whether you want to start your own business, expand your network, or explore joint ventures, being open to business opportunities can lead to exciting experiences and growth.

Industry Involvement: Do you want to become more actively involved in industry organisations or events? Engaging with professional associations, attending conferences, and participating in industry-related activities can help you expand your network, stay updated on industry trends, and build your professional reputation.

By carefully considering these essential aspects, such as your skills, interests, and values, you can gain a more precise and comprehensive understanding of your professional goals and aspirations. This self-reflection enables you to identify the steps and actions required to achieve them, empowering you to make meaningful progress. Additionally, by defining your networking objectives and establishing a targeted approach, you can tailor your networking efforts to align with your goals. Regularly assessing your progress will help you gauge whether you are moving closer to your desired outcomes and make any necessary adjustments.

Key Networking Metrics

There are several important metrics that you can utilise to evaluate the impact of your networking efforts effectively. These metrics can provide valuable insights into the effectiveness of your networking strategies, allowing you to assess the reach, engagement, and overall success of your networking initiatives. By carefully analysing these metrics, you can make informed decisions and optimise your networking approach for maximum impact and results.:

1. Network Growth

To effectively track the growth of your professional network, you can utilise platforms like LinkedIn. This powerful platform not only provides you with the number of connections you have, but it also offers valuable insights into the quality and diversity of your network. By monitoring the expansion of your connections and nurturing meaningful relationships, you can enhance your professional opportunities and stay ahead in your career journey.

2. Referrals

One effective way to gauge the effectiveness of your network is to measure the number of referrals or job opportunities that have come your way through it. By keeping a record of these referrals, you can gain valuable insights into your connections' value and impact. This data can help you further analyse the strength and potential of your network, enabling you to make informed decisions and foster meaningful relationships.

3. Information Gained

Take a moment to assess the valuable insights and knowledge you've gained through your network connections. Are you actively learning about the latest industry trends, discovering best practices to enhance your skills, or uncovering exciting career opportunities that could propel your professional journey to new heights? Embrace the power of your network and leverage it to expand your horizons and achieve your goals continuously.

4. Career Advancement

It is essential to track your career progression meticulously, documenting the significant milestones such as promotions, advancements, or any opportunities that have materialised through your professional connections. By keeping a record of these achievements, you can reflect upon your growth and success and use this valuable information to showcase your accomplishments to potential employers or collaborators.

5. Mentorship Relationships

You should take some time to reflect on and evaluate the quality and impact of your mentorship relationships. Consider the valuable guidance, support, and insights your mentors provided along your journey. Assess how their expertise and experience have influenced your growth and development. Recognise how their mentorship has contributed to your success and personal fulfilment.

6. Skills Acquired

Also, it is advised that you measure and evaluate the new skills or knowledge you have acquired directly from your diligent networking efforts. By assessing the specific areas of growth and improvement that have emerged from your networking endeavours, you can gain valuable insights into the impact and effectiveness of your proactive approach to expanding your professional horizons.

Self-Reflection

Regular self-reflection is crucial in evaluating your networking impact. Take a moment to pause and ponder. Ask yourself:

Have you ever evaluated whether your networking efforts align with your long-term goals and aspirations? It's essential to take a step back and assess if the connections you're making and the relationships you're building are helping you move closer to your desired future. Ensuring that your networking strategy is in sync with your aspirations can significantly enhance your chances of success in achieving your goals.

Have you found any specific connections or groups consistently proven exceptionally beneficial and supportive? These could be individuals or communities who have provided guidance, encouragement, and valuable resources to help you. Building strong relationships and finding supportive networks can significantly impact personal and professional growth.

You can implement several specific actions and strategies to enhance further and refine your networking approach. Firstly, you could actively seek networking opportunities, whether attending industry events, joining professional organisations, or participating in online networking communities. Additionally, you could nurture and maintain your existing network by regularly connecting with contacts, engaging in meaningful conversations, and offering support and assistance when needed. Furthermore, consider diversifying your networking efforts by exploring different industries or contacting individuals with diverse backgrounds and expertise. Continuously refining and expanding your networking approach can maximise your potential for success and create valuable connections to propel your professional growth.

You might get tremendously significant insights by venturing further into these thought-provoking questions and thoroughly analysing the complexities of your networking encounters. These insights, in turn, empower you to make informed decisions that can propel your personal and professional growth forward. Accepting this mentality of constant development and using your networking knowledge will undoubtedly pave the path to success in all aspects of your life.

Nurturing Your Network

It's important to remember that networking is a reciprocal process. Establishing and nurturing connections requires consistent effort and a sincere curiosity in others. Rather than viewing your contacts as means to an end, strive to cultivate authentic, lasting relationships built on mutual respect and support.

To build strong connections, make it a habit to check in with your contacts regularly. Please offer your support and assistance whenever possible, showing genuine interest in their lives, career journeys, and accomplishments. Doing so can foster deeper relationships and create mutual growth and success opportunities.

Take a moment to express heartfelt gratitude for the incredible opportunities and invaluable insights that your impressive network has graciously provided. Tell them how their exceptional guidance and unwavering support have profoundly influenced and contributed to your tremendous personal and professional growth journey.

Embrace a mindset of generosity and be ever ready to pay it forward by wholeheartedly supporting and uplifting others in their pursuit of goals and aspirations. Extend your vast expertise, abundant resources, and extensive network connections to empower and enable them to achieve remarkable success.

You'll cultivate a network beyond mere benefits by dedicating time and effort to nurturing genuine and meaningful connections. It will become a source of fulfilment, enriching your personal and professional life. The bonds you form through authenticity will provide support, inspiration, and opportunities for growth, fostering a network that genuinely adds value to your journey.

Adapting Your Strategy

If your networking efforts are not yielding the desired results, feel free to adapt your strategy. Take the opportunity to seek valuable feedback from mentors or experienced networkers who can provide insights and guidance tailored to your specific goals and challenges. Embrace the mindset of continuous improvement and be willing to explore and experiment with new approaches, techniques, and platforms.

One way to adapt your strategy is by diversifying your networking activities. Instead of solely relying on traditional events and conferences, consider joining online communities and participating in virtual networking opportunities. Your professional network will grow due to connecting with individuals from various sectors and places, creating new opportunities for learning and collaboration.

Additionally, it's essential to focus on building genuine and meaningful connections. Instead of approaching networking as a transactional process, take the time to establish rapport and cultivate relationships based on mutual trust and shared interests. It can lead to long-lasting partnerships and opportunities beyond just exchanging business cards.

Networking is a dynamic process that requires flexibility and adaptability. Stay open-minded and proactive in your quest for meaningful connections and opportunities. Continuously evaluate and refine your networking strategy based on feedback and insights gathered along the way. Doing so can increase your chances of achieving your networking goals and unlocking new professional opportunities.

In a case study that we will investigate, titled **"Effects of Networking on Career Success: A Longitudinal Study"**, authors Hans-Georg Wolff and Klaus Moser explore the significance of networking in shaping one's professional journey. Their findings reveal that networking efforts can substantially influence career progression. Individuals increase their chances of receiving job offers and promotions by actively engaging in networking activities. The researchers emphasise the importance of building strong connections, as these are more likely to provide valuable job leads and referrals.

The case study, **"The ROI of Networking"** by Ivan Misner focuses on the business perspective. The study highlights that businesses can achieve a significant return on investment through effective networking strategies. By actively engaging in networking activities, companies can generate new leads, build relationships with potential clients, and attract top talent. The study further emphasises that businesses that invest in networking training and programs are more likely to thrive and succeed in their respective industries.

Overall, these case studies underscore the crucial role of networking in personal and professional growth. They emphasise how networking facilitates career advancement and job satisfaction and increases earnings and business success. The chapter in your book highlighting the value of networking and how it can affect readers' lives and careers should use these findings.

Measuring the impact of your networking efforts is crucial to ensure that your connections genuinely contribute to your professional growth and help you achieve your goals. By setting clear and specific objectives, tracking relevant and meaningful metrics, and nurturing genuine and valuable relationships, you can fine-tune your networking strategy to maximise its effectiveness and ensure long-term success. Continuously assess and adapt your approach, keeping in mind that networking is not just about the quantity of connections you make but, more importantly, the quality and depth of those connections. Invest time and effort in building and nurturing relationships that truly matter and align with your aspirations. Remember, a solid and well-crafted network can open doors to new opportunities, provide support and guidance, and ultimately propel you towards your desired professional success.

Building a Sustainable Networking Routine

Developing and sustaining a sustainable networking routine is crucial to ensure your connections remain valuable and practical and thrive over the long run. This extensive chapter will cover the methods and approaches for creating and sustaining a regular networking schedule that advances your career goals and development and cultivates deep connections with like-minded people in your field. By implementing these techniques, you may build a strong network that leads to new possibilities, improves your reputation, and elevates your career.

Consistency Is Key

I have discussed this many times in this book. effective networking is not a one-time effort but a continuous and consistent practice. Incorporating networking into your daily, weekly, or monthly schedule is critical to establishing a sustainable networking routine. Doing so allows you to actively engage with industry peers, attend relevant events, and create meaningful connections. This proactive approach ensures you stay updated with the latest trends, exchange knowledge, and seize new opportunities. So, make networking a priority and watch as it opens doors to new collaborations, professional growth, and success.:

Daily Networking Routine

Networking is an indispensable skill for students that can open doors to numerous opportunities. A daily networking routine can aid in building fruitful relationships and enhance personal growth and career development. From attending workshops to engaging in online forums, students should incorporate networking into their everyday routine to reap its immense benefits.

Connect on social media: Dedicate a few minutes daily to connecting with professionals in your industry or field on popular social media platforms like LinkedIn or Twitter. Expanding your network allows you to gain insights, stay updated on industry trends, and build valuable relationships that can contribute to your professional growth.

Engage: Show your online presence by engaging with relevant posts or articles. Like, share, or comment on content that resonates with you or adds value to your network. It helps you stay connected and showcases your expertise and interests within your industry.

Respond to Messages: Regularly check and promptly respond to any networking messages or inquiries you receive. Engaging in meaningful conversations and building connections through personalised interactions can lead to new opportunities, collaborations, or partnerships.

Consistent and genuine engagement on social media can help you establish yourself as a knowledgeable professional while expanding your professional network.

Weekly Networking Routine

In today's connected world, networking is super important for students who want to succeed in their chosen fields. I can't stress enough how establishing a weekly networking routine can help them expand their professional network. Whether it's attending industry seminars or joining online discussion groups, incorporating these activities into their weekly schedule can open up incredible connections and opportunities.

Plan and Attend Events: Take the time to actively seek out local or virtual events, meetups, or webinars that align with your field of interest. Proactively schedule your attendance to stay up to date with the latest trends and network with like-minded professionals.

Follow-Up: After you've taken part in events or had discussions, it's really important to send follow-up messages to the new connections you've made. It's a great way to build stronger relationships and can open doors for collaboration or future opportunities. So don't forget to reach out - it can make a real difference!

Share Your Insights: You should embrace your expertise and contribute to the industry by writing and sharing insightful content. Whether through articles, blog posts, or thought pieces, sharing your knowledge can establish you as a thought leader and generate meaningful discussions within your professional community.

Monthly Networking Routine

Kickstarting a successful career begins with building meaningful connections. A monthly networking routine is invaluable for students to expand their professional horizons. Students can unlock opportunities that propel their careers forward by dedicating monthly time to attend industry events, engage in online forums, and connect with professionals.

Reach Out for Catchups: Why not take the chance to catch up with your existing network every month? It could be over a cup of coffee, a virtual video call, or even a leisurely walk. These catchup sessions are a great way to maintain and strengthen your relationships with your contacts. Let's keep those connections going strong!

Evaluate Your Progress: Set aside time to reflect on your networking goals and achievements over the past month. Assess the connections you've made, the knowledge you've gained, and the progress you've made towards your networking objectives. This self-reflection helps you identify areas for improvement and celebrate your successes.

Expand Your Network: Be bold, step out of your comfort zone, and seek new professionals or mentors to connect with. Attend networking events, join industry-related groups or communities, and leverage online platforms to find like-minded individuals. Building new relationships broadens your network, exposes you to fresh perspectives, and opens doors to exciting opportunities.

Building Your Networking Calendar

Creating a comprehensive calendar that outlines your networking activities for the entire month is highly recommended to ensure a consistent and effective networking routine. This calendar should include specific actions such as attending industry events, conferences, or seminars, reaching out to potential connections through personalised messages or emails, and even actively engaging with your network by regularly posting valuable content on platforms like LinkedIn or Twitter. By diligently scheduling and organising your networking efforts, you will significantly reduce the chances of overlooking or neglecting this critical aspect of professional growth, ultimately maximising your opportunities for meaningful connections and fruitful collaborations. Building and maintaining a robust network requires dedication, strategic planning, and consistent effort.

Setting Realistic Goals

Setting realistic goals that align with your objectives is essential as you establish your networking routine. Your dreams depend on the quantity of new contacts you hope to develop, the regularity of your exchanges, or even the volume of insightful material you intend to distribute. By defining clear and attainable goals within your available time and resources, you can effectively measure your progress and ensure you stay on track to build a successful network. So, take the time to plan, strategise, and watch your networking efforts yield fruitful results!

Monitoring Your Progress

Regularly assess your progress and the effectiveness of your networking routine. Take the time to reflect and ask yourself some crucial questions:

Are you consistently achieving your networking goals, or are there any specific areas that need improvement? It's important to reflect on your networking efforts and identify any potential challenges or opportunities for growth. By assessing and refining your approach, you can maximise your networking success and build valuable connections. Keep striving for improvement and watch your networking efforts flourish!

Are your professional connections gradually becoming more valuable and meaningful relationships? Are you actively cultivating strong and mutually beneficial relations that contribute to your growth and success in the long run? Building and nurturing such relationships can significantly enhance your professional journey and open doors to new opportunities.

Are you actively engaging in a continuous process of learning and personal growth through your daily interactions? Are you seeking opportunities to expand your insights, acquire new knowledge, and develop valuable skills to propel you forward on your journey of self-improvement and success? Embrace every chance to broaden your horizons, challenge your perspectives, and cultivate a lifelong learning and growth mindset.

Feel free to adjust your networking routine if you're not seeing the desired results. Stay receptive to discovering new methods, resources, or techniques that can assist you in reaching your goals. Networking is dynamic, and adapting and evolving along the way is essential.

Nurturing Meaningful Relationships

When establishing a sustainable networking routine, it's crucial to recognise the significance of nurturing meaningful, two-way relationships. Instead of just collecting contacts, prioritise the process of building authentic connections that go beyond surface-level interactions. Take the time to understand the needs and interests of individuals in your network and strive to provide value and support whenever possible. Doing so will create a robust and reliable network filled with genuine connections that can benefit you and others in the long run.

A sustainable networking routine is the bedrock of your professional growth and long-term success. By seamlessly integrating networking into your daily, weekly, and monthly activities, setting achievable goals, meticulously monitoring your progress, and actively nurturing meaningful relationships, you can ensure your network remains valuable and highly effective throughout your career trajectory. Networking should not be perceived as a mere task but rather as a continuous and enriching journey that opens many opportunities and fosters personal and professional growth when diligently managed and consistently cultivated. Whether it's forging new connections, fostering collaborations, or gaining industry insights, the power of networking is unparalleled. So, adopt this proactive attitude, put time and effort into creating and maintaining your network, and see how it may revolutionise your professional endeavour.

Networking Challenges and How to Overcome Them

Although networking is highly beneficial, it may be a challenging endeavour at times. This chapter will examine some of the most prevalent networking difficulties and propose practical solutions. By implementing these strategies, you can build and nurture a robust professional network, fostering meaningful connections to enhance your career growth and open doors to exciting opportunities. So, let's dive in and explore the intricacies of effective networking together!

Challenge 1: Overcoming Shyness and Social Anxiety

Networking, the process of connecting with new people, can be intimidating, especially for individuals who are naturally shy or experience social anxiety. However, you can overcome this challenge with a few strategies and make meaningful connections that benefit your personal and professional life. Here are some tips to help you navigate networking situations with confidence and ease:

Practice: Alright, let's start by gradually exposing yourself to low-pressure social situations. Think of small gatherings with friends or family, for example. Trust me, doing this will boost your confidence and help you grow more comfortable in social settings. You'll see, it's all about taking small steps and building up from there.

Set Realistic Goals: Instead of overwhelming yourself with the pressure to connect with a large group of people, focus on making one or two meaningful connections. Setting realistic goals allows you to engage in deeper conversations and establish more meaningful relationships.

Use Technology: Take use of the opportunities provided by technology to ease yourself into networking. Initial online interactions can be less intimidating, providing a stepping stone to in-person networking. Connect with others in your industry using social media platforms, professional networking websites, and virtual events.

Seek Support: If networking feels daunting, consider joining networking groups or attending events with a friend or colleague. Having someone by your side can provide emotional support and make the experience more enjoyable. You can encourage and motivate each other, boosting your confidence and making networking a positive experience.

It is possible to gain proficiency in networking over time. With practice, realistic goals, the use of technology, and the support of others, you can become more confident and effective in your networking efforts.

Challenge 2: Making Time for Networking

In today's fast-paced world, where busy schedules consume our time, many people find it challenging to carve out dedicated moments for networking. Whether due to work commitments, personal responsibilities, or simply the overwhelming demands of daily life, nurturing professional connections can often take a backseat. However, by recognising the importance of networking and implementing effective strategies to overcome this obstacle, individuals can unlock valuable opportunities for growth, collaboration, and success.:

Prioritise: Networking is super important, so don't forget to make it a priority alongside your other professional activities. Building a solid network can open up doors to new opportunities, collaborations, and valuable connections in your industry. Make sure to actively engage and nurture your network because it can contribute to your professional growth.

Incorporate into Daily Routine: Make networking a daily habit, whether connecting on social media, reading industry news, or sending a quick message to a connection. Integrating networking activities into your daily routine lets you stay updated with the latest trends, expand your knowledge, and forge meaningful relationships with like-minded professionals. Consistency is vital to building a robust network supporting your career aspirations.

Time Management: Efficiently manage your time by setting specific networking goals and allocating dedicated time for them. Identify the networking activities that align with your objectives and prioritise them accordingly. Effective time management will ensure you maximise your networking efforts without neglecting other essential tasks, whether attending industry events, participating in online communities, or scheduling one-on-one meetings.

Combine Activities: Attend networking events that align with your interests, such as combining a hobby with networking. It can make networking more enjoyable and increases the chances of connecting with individuals who share similar passions. By integrating networking into activities, you enjoy, you can effortlessly expand your network while engaging in something you love.

Investing time and effort in networking may pay off handsomely throughout your career. You may optimise the benefits of networking and pave the road to professional success by incorporating these methods into your approach.

Challenge 3: Building Confidence

Building confidence in networking can be a significant challenge, especially for those new to the field or naturally introverted. However, by implementing a few proven strategies and techniques, individuals can overcome this hurdle and develop the necessary skills to thrive in networking situations. Whether practising active listening, seeking out networking opportunities, or honing your elevator pitch, these strategies can provide a solid foundation for building confidence and making meaningful connections in the professional world.

Practice Elevator Pitches: Make sure to take the time to practice and polish your elevator pitch. It's all about being able to confidently present yourself and your ideas in any situation. Mastering your pitch will help you grab the attention of others and leave a lasting impression. So go ahead, rehearse, refine, and capture those opportunities!

Preparation: Thoroughly research event topics or attendees beforehand to enhance networking success. This will provide valuable insights to help you engage in more informed and meaningful conversations. By being well-prepared, you will feel more confident and be able to contribute to discussions easily.

Learn from Mistakes: Don't worry about networking missteps, they're valuable learning experiences, not setbacks. Every interaction, even if it doesn't go as planned, can give you insights into areas for improvement. Trust me, by having a growth mindset and seeing mistakes as opportunities for growth, you'll keep refining your networking skills and get better at building connections.

Visualise Success: Get mentally prepared for networking interactions by picturing yourself acing it! Imagine confidently chatting away, forging meaningful connections, and leaving a positive impression. This little visualization exercise can amp up your confidence and set the right intentions for your networking adventures. You got this!

Challenge 4: Fear of Rejection

The fear of rejection is a common hurdle many encounters when networking. Putting yourself out there and facing the possibility of being turned down or ignored can be daunting. However, understanding how to confront and overcome this fear is crucial for building meaningful connections and advancing professionally. You can navigate networking situations confidently and resiliently by developing strategies to manage rejection, such as reframing it as a learning opportunity or focusing on your value. Accepting rejection as a normal part of the process might ultimately lead to growth and success in your networking efforts.

Shift Your Mindset: It's really important to change your mindset and understand that rejection is normal and expected when it comes to networking. It doesn't define your worth or abilities at all. Instead, look at it as a chance to learn and grow.

Focus on Quality Over Quantity: Instead of trying to impress everyone you meet, try focusing on building a few meaningful connections. Take the time to really get to know people, understand their needs and interests, and offer genuine support and value. It's all about creating those personal connections and making a positive impact.

Seek Feedback: Don't hesitate to ask for feedback if a connection doesn't achieve the desired outcome. Politely inquire about ways to improve or areas you may need to improve. Constructive feedback can provide valuable insights and help you refine your networking approach.

Diversify Your Approach: If one networking strategy isn't yielding the desired results, don't hesitate to try a different approach. Explore various avenues, such as attending industry events, joining online communities, or leveraging social media platforms. By diversifying your strategy, you can connect with a broader range of people and expand your networking opportunities.

Challenge 5: Maintaining Professionalism

You are maintaining professionalism while networking is essential and critical in building strong and lasting connections. When engaging with others in a professional setting, being mindful of your communication style, body language, and overall demeanour is crucial. Presenting yourself confidently and respectfully can create a positive impression and establish credibility. Remember to actively listen, ask thoughtful questions, and show genuine interest in others' perspectives and experiences. Doing so can foster meaningful relationships that may lead to new opportunities and collaborations. So, the next time you find yourself networking, remember these tips to easily navigate the challenge of maintaining professionalism.

Listen Actively: When engaging with someone, make a conscious effort to listen to them actively. Show genuine interest by paying close attention to what they are saying. Additionally, ask open-ended questions to encourage further conversation and to demonstrate that you value their thoughts and opinions.

Observe Social Norms: When interacting with others, it is essential to be mindful of cultural and social norms. By being aware of these norms, you can ensure your interactions are respectful and considerate. It includes understanding appropriate greetings, gestures, and customs in different settings and cultures.

Practice Good Communication: Effective communication is critical in any interaction. Use clear and concise language to convey your thoughts and ideas. Maintain appropriate eye contact to show attentiveness and interest. Additionally, be aware of your body language, which can express messages and emotions. Being mindful of these aspects can help create a positive and engaging communication experience.

Follow-up: After attending networking events, it is essential to send a follow-up message to express gratitude and maintain professionalism. It could include thanking the person for their time, referencing something specifically discussed, and telling your interest in future collaborations or conversations. Following up not only shows your appreciation but also helps to build and strengthen professional relationships.

Challenge 6: Navigating Awkward Situations

Awkward situations can sometimes unexpectedly arise during networking events, leaving us momentarily unsure how to navigate them gracefully. Knowing how to handle such situations with tact and poise can create a positive and lasting impression, whether it's a mismatched introduction or a conversation that takes an unexpected turn. By staying calm, actively listening, and responding thoughtfully, you can effectively navigate these moments, turning them into opportunities for growth and building meaningful connections. So, the next time an awkward situation arises during networking, remember these tips and approach them confidently.

Graceful Exits: When finding yourself in an uncomfortable conversation, gracefully exit by expressing your intention to meet other attendees. Politely excuse yourself, mentioning that there are other people you would like to catch up with or engage in conversation.

Recovery: If you make a mistake or say something awkward during a conversation, acknowledge it with a touch of humour. Lightly address the situation, comment lightly, and move on smoothly. Remember, everyone makes slip-ups from time to time, and it's how we handle them that truly matters.

Redirecting: If a conversation takes an uncomfortable turn, skilfully steer it toward a more neutral topic. Look for common interests or areas everyone can contribute to, creating a more inclusive and enjoyable atmosphere. You can maintain a positive and engaging interaction for everyone involved by redirecting the conversation.

As we conclude this chapter, we will finally explore three insightful case studies on the Challenges of Networking. The article **"An Introvert's Guide to Networking"** by Lisa Petrilli, published in Harvard Business Review, emphasises the importance of networking, particularly for introverts. Petrilli shares her personal experiences and discusses her initial aversion to networking early in her career. Petrilli's insights provide valuable guidance for introverts navigating the networking landscape. The article underscores that while networking might seem daunting for introverts, it is a crucial aspect of career development.

The second case study, **"The Art of Virtual Networking"** by Soulaima Gourani, sheds light on the unique difficulties of virtual networking. Building rapport and trust becomes more challenging due to the absence of in-person cues and the potential for distractions. However, leveraging virtual platforms like LinkedIn and video conferencing tools can enhance networking success. Creating a dedicated workspace for virtual networking minimises distractions and maintains focus.

Find the whole case study on the internet or in your library. These case studies offer valuable insights into common networking challenges and provide strategies for overcoming them.

Networking challenges are a natural and inevitable part of the process. However, with the right strategies and a positive attitude, you can overcome them and open doors to new opportunities. Shyness, for instance, can make networking demoralising. Still, gradually stepping out of your comfort zone and engaging in small conversations can build confidence and establish meaningful connections. Time constraints are another hurdle, but you can make it a seamless part of your routine by prioritising networking events and setting aside dedicated time for relationship-building. Confidence is critical, and by focusing on your strengths and unique qualities, you can exude a genuine aura that attracts others. Overcoming the fear of rejection may seem challenging but remember that every interaction is an opportunity to learn and grow. Professionalism is crucial; you can leave a lasting impression by maintaining a polished and respectful demeanour. Awkward circumstances may emerge, but you may successfully traverse them by retaining a sense of humour and agility. Recognising and confronting these issues can help you become a more prosperous and confident networker, building deeper relationships, and unlocking bigger chances in your career path.

The Future of Networking

In today's fast-paced world, the landscape of networking is in a constant state of flux. To ensure the longevity and success of your professional network, it is crucial to stay ahead of the curve. In this final chapter, we will dig into the exciting domain of networking's future. We will explore emerging trends, cutting-edge technologies, and innovative strategies that will enable you to adapt and thrive in this ever-evolving domain. By equipping yourself with the knowledge and skills needed to remain relevant and practical, you will be well-prepared to navigate the dynamic world of networking with confidence and success.

Understanding Technology

Technology has revolutionised our network, transforming it into a seamless and interconnected experience. With the constant advancements in technology, it is crucial to understand how to leverage it effectively for successful networking. By embracing the power of technology, we can expand our reach, connect with like-minded professionals, and tap into a global network of opportunities. From utilising social media platforms to attending virtual networking events, there are countless ways to harness the potential of technology and elevate our networking game. So, let's dive deeper into technological networking and unlock its full potential for professional growth and success.

Leverage social media: In today's digital age, staying updated on new social media platforms and features is crucial. By doing so, you can effectively connect with a broader audience and tap into new opportunities for networking and collaboration.

Virtual Events: With the rise of virtual networking events and webinars, the world has become more connected. Embrace these virtual platforms as they provide a convenient and efficient way to expand your professional network and gain valuable insights from industry leaders.

AI and Automation: Take advantage of the power of AI-driven tools in your networking efforts. These innovative tools can help you discover new connections, automate follow-ups, and track your networking progress. By leveraging AI and automation, you can optimise your networking strategy and make the most out of your interactions.

Online Platforms: LinkedIn is the go-to professional networking platform, so don't limit yourself to just one platform. Explore niche platforms that are specific to your industry or area of interest. These platforms can offer unique networking opportunities and allow you to connect with like-minded professionals who share your passion and expertise. By diversifying your online presence, you can maximise your networking potential and expand your professional horizons.

Diversifying Networking Strategies

Diversifying your techniques is critical for staying ahead in networking and maintaining a competitive advantage. You may broaden your network and open doors to new prospects by experimenting with different tactics and techniques, such as attending industry events, utilising social media platforms, and developing solid relationships. Adopting a diverse strategy will not only increase your reach. Still, it will also position you to respond to shifting dynamics in the networking ecosystem. So, to succeed in the ever-changing networking world, keep discovering, trying, and adapting.

Hybrid Networking: You should look into the power of hybrid networking, where we combine the best of both worlds: online and in-person interactions. Online networking gives you a wider reach and convenience, while in-person networking allows for genuine connections and deeper relationships. It's like having the best of both worlds!

Global Reach: You should expand your horizons and transcend geographical boundaries to seek connections and opportunities worldwide. Embrace the diversity and richness of different cultures and perspectives, opening doors to new collaborations and growth.

Content Sharing: You can establish yourself as a trusted authority in your field by creating and sharing valuable content. Whether it's insightful articles, engaging videos, or thought-provoking podcasts, consistently sharing practical knowledge will position you as a go-to resource in your industry.

Industry Participation: You should actively participate in industry-specific groups, forums, and online communities to stay up to date with the latest trends and developments. Engage in meaningful discussions, share your expertise, and learn from fellow professionals to enhance your knowledge and expand your network.

Networking in the Gig Economy

With the gig economy on the rise, networking in this dynamic landscape involves connecting with a diverse range of professionals, including freelancers, independent contractors, and remote workers. Individuals can tap into a vast talent pool and expertise by engaging with this vibrant community, fostering collaborative opportunities and innovative partnerships. Embracing the flexibility and entrepreneurial spirit of the gig economy opens doors to new possibilities. It expands professional networks, paving the way for success in this evolving work environment.

Collaboration Opportunities: Welcome the gig economy by collaborating with independent professionals on projects or ventures. It allows you to tap into a diverse pool of talent and expertise. It fosters creativity and innovation through collaborative problem-solving.

Remote Networking: Expand your network by connecting with individuals from diverse locations and backgrounds. Engage in virtual meetups, webinars, and online communities to establish meaningful connections, share insights, and gain fresh perspectives. Networking across borders has always been challenging!

Skill Exchange: Leverage the gig economy to exchange skills and expertise with others. Whether through mentorship programs, skill-sharing platforms, or project-based collaborations, the gig economy provides ample opportunities to learn from and teach others, fostering continuous growth and development.

By taking advantage of these chances, you may prosper in the gig economy, make crucial contacts, and expand your skill set.

The Role of Lifelong Learning

In the ever-evolving networking landscape, the future strongly emphasises the immense value of lifelong learning. As technology advances and industries rapidly change, individuals who embrace continuous learning will stay relevant and gain a competitive edge. By acquiring new knowledge and skills and staying updated with the latest trends, professionals can confidently adapt to the dynamic networking landscape. The future of networking is an exciting journey of growth and endless opportunities for those committed to expanding their knowledge horizons.

Stay Informed: Keep updating your knowledge and skills by staying on top of industry trends, attending workshops and conferences, and exploring online learning platforms. It'll make sure you stay valuable and well-informed, with the latest insights and expertise.

Mentorship: Let's prioritise mentorship, both as mentors and mentees, to foster learning and personal growth. As a mentor, I'm here to share my experiences and guidance with you, helping you navigate your career path. As a mentee, don't hesitate to seek guidance from experienced professionals who can provide valuable insights and advice, accelerating your professional development.

Adaptation: Stay open to adapting your networking strategies as industries and technologies evolve. It's like keeping up with the latest trends and being flexible to make the most of your connections. Stay agile and proactive in embracing new tools and platforms to enhance your networking efforts. Whether leveraging social media, attending virtual events, or exploring innovative networking techniques, being adaptable will ensure you stay ahead in the ever-changing networking landscape.

One of the exciting articles I found will be helpful to you is "A Better Approach to Networking". This article by Christie Hunter Arscott in Harvard Business Review provides a better approach to networking. It suggests focusing on what you will ask, not what you will say, and practising moving from small to deep talk.

The future of networking is dynamic and ever evolving, driven by advancements in technology, the increasing diversification of strategies, and the changing nature of work in our interconnected world. To survive and thrive in this rapidly changing landscape, embracing technology as a powerful tool for connectivity and collaboration is crucial. Additionally, diversifying your networking strategies will allow you to tap into different industries, communities, and perspectives, expanding your network and opening new opportunities.

In this age of the gig economy, it is essential to navigate the ever-changing landscape of freelance and contract work. Cultivating a solid online presence, leveraging social media platforms, and actively participating in online communities relevant to your field can help you connect with potential clients, collaborators, and mentors.

Furthermore, lifelong learning has become a fundamental aspect of successful networking. By continuously updating your skills, staying abreast of industry trends, and actively seeking new knowledge, you can position yourself as a valuable and adaptable professional in networking.

Networking is no longer just about making connections today but about your ability to adapt and evolve as the networking landscape continues to shift. By remaining flexible, embracing change, and being open to new opportunities, you can build and maintain a thriving professional network that enhances your career prospects and fosters personal growth.

The key to navigating the gig economy, prioritising lifelong learning, and cultivating meaningful relationships in this dynamic future of networking is your willingness to embrace technology, diversify your methods, negotiate the gig economy, and develop meaningful connections. With these pillars in place, you'll be well-equipped to navigate the ever-changing networking landscape and discover new opportunities for success and growth.

Final Thoughts and Looking Ahead

As we end our journey through the dynamic landscape of networking, let's take a moment to reflect on the major themes and key learnings we've explored. We have seen how technology, diversity, the gig economy, and lifelong learning are profoundly reshaping networking. Each of these themes is not an isolated trend but a vital part of a bigger picture that's shaping the future of networking.

According to a report by McKinsey Global Institute, freelance work is on the rise, with up to 162 million people in Europe and the United States or 20 to 30 per cent of the working-age population engaged in independent work. This growth is a testament to the power of the gig economy, which provides unprecedented opportunities for professionals to connect, collaborate, and share their skills globally.

Yet, navigating the gig economy is about more than finding freelance work. It's about leveraging technology and digital platforms to build a robust online presence, engage with relevant communities, and stay informed about industry trends. A LinkedIn survey found that 85% of all jobs are filled via networking, underscoring the importance of maintaining an active online presence.

The diversification of networking strategies is another crucial aspect of this evolving landscape. No longer confined to industry-specific events or traditional meetups, networking has expanded into various channels and platforms. From online forums and social media to webinars and virtual events, the possibilities for connecting with professionals from multiple fields are virtually limitless.

Continuous learning is the glue that binds all these themes together. In a fast-paced world where industries and technologies constantly evolve, embracing lifelong learning is not just optional, it's essential. According to a report by the World Economic Forum, by 2022, no less than 54% of all employees will require significant re- and upskilling. The key to networking success is adapting to these changes, staying informed about industry trends, and continuously acquiring new skills.

As we look ahead, it's clear that even more exciting trends will shape the future of networking. The advent of 5G technology will revolutionise our network by enabling faster and more efficient data transfer. The rise of artificial intelligence will empower professionals to automate and streamline networking tasks, from scheduling meetups to personalising communication. And the continuous evolution of social media will create new platforms and opportunities for professionals to connect in real-time across borders.

The future of networking is not just about adapting to these changes and embracing them with open arms. It's about transforming challenges into opportunities, pushing boundaries, and daring to explore uncharted territories. Above all, it's about realising that networking is not just a professional tool but a lifelong learning, growth, and personal enrichment journey.

As we wrap up this journey, remember that the future of networking lies in your hands. It's up to you to shape, mould, and make the most of it. Embrace the gig economy, leverage technology, diversify your networking strategies, and prioritise lifelong learning. By doing so, you'll succeed in networking and create opportunities for others to thrive.

Let this book guide you as you navigate the dynamic landscape of networking. Use the insights, tools, and strategies it provides to build a professional network that reflects your aspirations, values, and unique perspective. And most importantly, remember that networking is more than a strategy—it's a mindset, a lifestyle, and a commitment to lifelong learning and growth.

In the powerful words of inspirational author Roy T. Bennett, "Be the kind of person who dares to face life's challenges and overcome them rather than dodging them." As you venture into the future of networking, let this be your guiding mantra. Let every challenge serve as a stepping stone, every setback as a learning opportunity, and every success as a reminder of your resilience and adaptability.

Thank you for joining me on this remarkable journey through the future of networking. As we conclude, remember that this is not the end but the beginning of your unique networking journey - a journey filled with endless opportunities, profound discoveries, and inspiring connections. Here's to a future of networking as diverse, dynamic, and delightful as the professionals who shape it.

*** THE END ***

About the Author

Sanath Nair is not just a seasoned sales and marketing professional, but a dynamic force in the industry with a career that spans over two decades collaborating with some of the world's most esteemed teams and companies, adding a wealth of experience to his repertoire. His academic journey, which includes a bachelor's degree in production engineering and a master's degree in international business, has laid a robust foundation for his professional success.

His debut book, **"Corporate Transition: An Essential Guide for Academic Graduates,"** has been met with resounding praise from students and faculty members across the globe, marking his entry into the literary world.

Beyond the confines of his professional life, Sanath is an ardent writer. He spends his leisure time nurturing this passion, maintaining a personal blog aptly titled 'Fresher Blog.' His insightful writings, which reflect his depth of knowledge and unique perspective, can be found on his blog. For those interested in exploring his work further, the link is provided in his book.

www.ingramcontent.com/pod-product-compliance
Lightning Source LLC
Chambersburg PA
CBHW072206290526
45794CB00004B/1668